101 Questions & Answers on ANGELS AND DEVILS

Irene Nowell, OSB

Paulist Press
New York / Mahwah, NJ

Cover and book design by Lynn Else

Library of Congress Cataloging-in-Publication Data

Nowell, Irene, 1940–
101 questions & answers on angels and devils / Irene Nowell.
p. cm.
ISBN 978-0-8091-4694-9 (alk. paper)
1. Angels—Catholic Church—Miscellanea. 2. Demonology—Catholic Church—Miscellanea. 3. Catholic Church—Doctrines—Miscellanea. I. Title. II. Title: 101 questions and answers on angels and devils. III. Title: One hundred and one questions & answers on angels and devils. IV. Title: One hundred one questions & answers on angels and devils.
BT966.3.N69 2010
235′.3—dc22

2010033671

Published by Paulist Press
997 Macarthur Boulevard
Mahwah, New Jersey 07430

www.paulistpress.com

Printed and bound in the
United States of America

Contents

PART FOUR: ANGELS IN OTHER TRADITIONS

Dedication

To Father Lawrence Boadt, CSP (1942–2010)—
a careful, creative scholar and a good friend

Preface

I grew up with as much confidence in the existence of angels as in the reality of my nextdoor neighbors. My mother called on the angels frequently, not only for protection but also to help her find what she had lost. Their most dramatic response was the return of a pair of gloves that she had left in a restaurant in Santa Fe to our home in Iowa. In elementary school the Visitation Sisters who taught me had a practice of stopping class every hour for a brief prayer, and each prayer time was dedicated to one of the choirs of angels. When I entered monastic life, I was comforted when we sang at a sister's funeral, "May the angels take you into paradise." So it comes as no surprise that the topic of my doctoral dissertation was the book of Tobit, in which the archangel Raphael plays a major role. I still pray to the angels and love to ask people if they have ever experienced the presence and aid of an angel.

Awareness of supernatural spiritual beings has been a part of human experience from the beginning. Some ancient peoples called these beings "gods" and both feared and honored them. In the three major religions descended from Abraham—Judaism, Christianity, and Islam—belief in only one God led to the understanding of these spiritual beings as subordinate to God but often more powerful than human beings. Those who are good have come to be called "angels" and those who are evil "devils" or "demons."

Angels seem to be everywhere in American culture, especially but not only around Christmastime. There are angel pins, angel cartoons, angel cards, pictures of angels, and many books about angels. Demons and devils lurk in the dark corners of our common consciousness too. Sometimes they are portrayed comically, but often their function is to terrify us into the realization of overwhelming evil.

So why another book about these good and evil spirits? This book is intended as a handy and carefully researched guide to belief in angels and devils throughout the millennia. Who and what are angels? What do they do for us? Should we be afraid of Satan and his demons? How do they afflict us? I have given attention to documents of major religious traditions, especially the Bible and the Qur'an, and to the portrayal of these spiritual beings in art and literature. My primary purpose in gathering all this information, however, is to enlighten our own experience as we strive to turn more and more away from evil and toward good. May the angels defend us from evil and lead us securely on the path to God.

Irene Nowell, OSB

PART ONE

Angels

1. What is an angel?

An angel is a spiritual being, created by God, whose sole purpose is to praise God and mediate between God and humanity. Angels are like us in that they are spiritual, but not like us because we have material bodies and they do not. Angels want to help us and want to bring us closer to God. Belief in angels is age-old and founded on reliable sources.

2. Where do we learn about angels?

We learn about angels from Scripture and tradition. Angels appear throughout Scripture, from the earliest writings in Genesis and Exodus to the latest books in the New Testament such as Revelation. Angels continue to be significant in Jewish works that were not included in the Bible and in the biblical commentaries and preaching of early Christian writers. Belief in angels is also stated in the official teachings of the Catholic Church, including documents from church councils and the *Catechism of the Catholic Church.*

3. What angels do we meet in the Old Testament?

The Old Testament has many stories about angels. Throughout the stories in Genesis, angels are helpful to the ancestors. When Hagar, the mother of Abraham's oldest son, is banished to the desert, an angel comforts her and shows her a source of life-giving water (Gen 16:7–12; 21:14–19). An angel stops Abraham's hand when he is about to sacrifice his son Isaac (Gen 22:10–12). When Abraham sends a servant to find a wife for Isaac, an angel guides him and protects him (Gen 24:40). Isaac's son Jacob is reassured by angels when he is forced to leave home after he steals his father's blessing from his older brother (Gen 28:12).

Angels continue to help people become aware of God's presence and God's call in their lives. An angel appears to Moses in a burning bush so that Moses can hear God calling him to lead his people out of Egypt (Exod 3:2). Centuries later, when God's people are being harassed by the Midianites, an angel brings God's call to Gideon (Judg 6:20–22). The most extensive Old Testament story concerning angels is that of the archangel Raphael, who plays a major role in the story of Tobit. God sent Raphael to bring all sorts of blessings to two families: guidance and protection, instruction and inspiration. He is even a matchmaker! Watch for angels throughout the Old Testament! They are shy and often disappear as the story gets underway, but if you pay attention you will find them everywhere.

4. We all know and love the story of the angels who announce the birth of Jesus to the shepherds in the field. Where else in the New Testament do we find angels?

Angels are very busy in the New Testament. The good news of Jesus' upcoming birth is announced to both Mary (Luke 1:26–32) and Joseph (Matt 1:20) by an angel. Joseph seems to have a special relationship with angels, since an angel also comes to warn him of Herod's intended murder of the baby (Matt 2:13). Angels comfort Jesus after the devil tempts him (Matt 4:11) and strengthen him as he agonizes over his impending passion (Luke 22:43). When Jesus rises from the dead, angels tell the women who come to the tomb to bring the news to the disciples (Matt 28:5–7; Luke 24:23).

After the resurrection the disciples rely on angels for many things. When they are imprisoned, angels sometimes rescue them (Acts 5:19; 12:7–11). Angels send them off to meet people who want to know more about Jesus: Philip is sent to help the Ethiopian eunuch (Acts 8:26) and Peter is sent to bring the good news to the centurion Cornelius (Acts 10:22). Just as an angel strengthened Jesus before his passion, an angel comes to encourage Paul when he is on his way to Rome, where he will be martyred (Acts 27:23).

Throughout the Book of Revelation, angels are major participants in the events of the last days before the end of the world (see, for example, Revelation 7—10).

5. Did the concept of angels develop and change in biblical times?

Yes. In the oldest biblical passages, for example in Genesis and Exodus, it is difficult to distinguish between an ordinary human messenger and an angel as a spiritual being. The same Hebrew word, *mal'ak*, is used for both. After the Babylonian Exile in the sixth century BCE, the understanding of angels as spiritual beings became stronger. Some of this development came from Persian influence with its dualistic belief in good and evil powers, since the Jews were ruled by Persia from 539 to 333 BCE. The worldview that we call "apocalyptic" also played a part. Apocalyptic writings like the Book of Daniel told stories of superhuman spiritual beings such as angels and devils who interpreted and affected human history for good or for ill. This apocalyptic worldview is represented in the New Testament in the Book of Revelation.

6. What early sources *not* from the Bible have become part of our tradition about angels?

Stories of angels—good and bad—are found in many Jewish works written in the last centuries BCE and the early centuries of the common era, from about 200 BCE to about 100 CE. The terms that refer to these books are rather confusing, since different religious traditions use different terms. For the sake of simplicity, we will refer to these books that are not included in any canon of Scripture—Catholic, Protestant, or Jewish—as pseudepigrapha (meaning "written under another name"). The Books of Enoch, the Book of Jubilees, and the Life of Adam and Eve are all pseudepigrapha.

7. Can you tell me more about these Books of Enoch? Who was Enoch?

Enoch is a mysterious figure. He is mentioned only briefly in Genesis: "Thus all the days of Enoch were three hundred sixty-five years. Enoch walked with God; then he was no more, because God took him" (Gen 5:23–24). Just as people at the end of the Old Testament period became very interested in Elijah because there was no report of his death, so they also began to wonder about Enoch. What happened when "God took him"? Several writers ventured an opinion. There are three works that bear the name of this man who "walked with God" (Gen 5:24). First Enoch is the longest. Its five sections were written at different times from about the third century BCE to the first century CE. First Enoch is the most helpful for us in understanding the tradition about angels. Second Enoch describes the seven heavens and the roles of the angels in each. In this book, Enoch is taken through the seven heavens, and when he arrives in the seventh heaven the archangel Michael is told to take off his earthly clothing, anoint him with oil, and dress him in "clothes of glory" (2 Enoch 22.8). So he becomes one of the angels. In Third Enoch we are told the story of Rabbi Ishmael, who is guided through the various levels of heaven by Enoch, now called the angel Metatron (3 Enoch 4.2–3).

8. What about the other books you mentioned: Jubilees and the Life of Adam and Eve? Do they tell the same stories?

The pseudepigraphal Book of Jubilees, which was written in the mid-second century BCE, is an interpretation of the biblical story from Adam to Moses, told from the viewpoint of biblical law and organized to fit the major religious festivals of the Jewish calendar. That is why it is called "Jubilees." It tells a story of creation similar to Genesis 1, but it also includes a description of God's creation of the angels and an instruction on the importance of

Sabbath. The fall of Adam and Eve and the murder of Abel by Cain are recounted as in Genesis. But a story is added reporting the death of Adam and the death of Cain in retribution for the murder of his brother. Jubilees says he was killed when his house fell on him. Jubilees also tells stories of Noah and the flood and of God's covenant with Abraham and the birth of Isaac. But again the story is expanded. Rebecca doesn't only tell Jacob how to steal Esau's blessing (see Genesis 27), but she also pronounces a long blessing over him. The book ends with a description of the laws for Passover and Sabbath. Throughout the Book of Jubilees attention is given to angels and demons: What do they do? How do they relate to God and human beings?

The Life of Adam and Eve, written around the first century CE, is a "midrash," a story told to fill in the gaps in the biblical narrative. It includes a story of Satan's fall, which is not in Scripture, and an elaboration on the story of his tempting human beings. It also fills in another gap. Haven't you wondered what happened to Adam and Eve *after* they were expelled from Eden? The Bible doesn't tell us much, but the Life of Adam and Eve gives us more detail.

9. Are the angels created beings like we are?

Yes. The angels are not infinite, like God, but are creatures of God. The church has always affirmed this. The Fourth Lateran Council (1215) puts it this way: God, "from the beginning of time and by His omnipotent power made from nothing creatures both spiritual and corporeal, angelic and mundane, and then human, as it were, common, composed of spirit and body" (Canon 1 of the Fourth Lateran Council). The decree *Dei Filius* of Vatican Council I (1870) repeats this same teaching (chap. 1, par. 3). Early Christian writers agree that the angels were created, but they disagree about *when* this happened, whether it was before the material universe was created or at the same time. The great thirteenth-century theologian St. Thomas Aquinas regards it more probable that the angels were created at the same time as material creatures.

10. How many angels are there?

The number of angels is beyond imagining. In the Old Testament, Daniel sees "a thousand thousands," even "ten thousand times ten thousand" present and serving God in the heavenly court (Dan 7:10). In the corresponding vision of God's court in the New Testament, many angels surround God's throne along with the living creatures and the elders. "They numbered myriads of myriads and thousands of thousands" (Rev 5:11). Jesus declares to those who come to arrest him that he can appeal to the Father who will send "more than twelve legions of angels" to defend him (Matt 26:53).

A common Old Testament name for God, "Lord of hosts" (Hebrew *yhwh sabaoth*), may also suggest the great number of angels. Hosts means "armies," and the angels in the Lord's armies are innumerable (see Ps 68:18; Matt 26:53). Thomas Aquinas says that the angels "exist in exceeding great number," far greater than we can understand.

11. Why did God create angels? What is their essential function?

St. Augustine points out that the term *angel*, which means "messenger," identifies *one* of the ministries of angels, but that their essential function is to be attendants at God's throne. Nonetheless, their ministry as messengers is very important to us. Scripture tells us that they are intermediaries between God and us, symbolized by Jacob's vision of the stairway between earth and heaven with angels ascending and descending (Gen 28:12). In this relationship to us, angels are mediators of prayer, guardians, messengers, and guides for human beings. They also have the power to carry out God's will by affecting the natural world.

12. What does it mean that angels are attendants at God's throne? How do they minister in God's presence?

Angels stand in God's presence, ready to do whatever God asks. The archangel Raphael identifies himself as "one of the seven angels who stand ready and enter before the glory of the Lord" (Tob 12:15; see Rev 8:2). They see God's face (Matt 18:10) and the wonder of God's presence inspires them to praise God continually. The visionary in the Book of Revelation reports that he saw the angels fall on their faces in reverent worship (Rev 7:11; see Ps 97:7). He also heard them singing God's praise "with full voice" (Rev 5:11–12; see 7:12). In the Psalms we enlist the angels to help us praise God: "Bless the Lord, O you his angels, you mighty ones who do his bidding" (Ps 103:20; see Pss 29:1; 148:2; Dan 3:58). The shepherds who are summoned by an angel to go to Bethlehem to see the newborn Christ hear a "multitude of the heavenly host" praising God (Luke 2:13–14).

In the Old Testament the angels also function as God's council. In the earlier texts these councilors are assumed to be other gods, but in the sixth century BCE, when God's people realized fully that not only was their God the most powerful but that their God was the only God, then God's councilors came to be understood as angels. The psalmist praises God as without equal "in the council of the holy ones" (Ps 89:5–8). God exercises judgment in the midst of the "divine council" (Ps 82:1). In the Book of Job, the "heavenly beings" (angels) come to present themselves before God, presumably to confer about what is happening on earth (Job 1:6; 2:1). The prophet Micaiah ben Imlah has a vision of the Lord consulting the "host of heaven" all around him concerning what to do with King Ahab. An angel, a "spirit," volunteers to deceive Ahab and is sent by the Lord to carry it out (1 Kings 22:19–22). So the angels, although they stand in God's presence, are also very involved with happenings on earth.

13. Does that mean that the angels are not only paying attention to God, but are also paying attention to us? How does that affect us? Do they help us pray?

Angels are very much concerned about our prayer. In the Book of Tobit the archangel Raphael says that when Tobit and Sarah prayed for relief from their suffering he was the one "who brought and read the record of [their] prayer before the glory of the Lord" (Tob 12:12). The Book of Revelation gives a more elaborate description of angels mediating human prayers. An angel with a golden censer stands at the golden altar before God's throne and offers incense "with the prayers of all the saints"; the prayers rise before God with the incense (Rev 8:3–4). In another passage the incense itself is said to be "the prayers of the saints" (Rev 5:8). Thus the angels seem to be making possible what we ask in Psalm 141: "Let my prayer be counted as incense before you, and the lifting up of my hands as an evening sacrifice" (Ps 141:2). It is a reassuring thought, when we wonder if our prayers are unworthy of God, to remember that the angels are carrying them to God's throne.

14. Angels are supposed to be messengers of God, aren't they? What kind of messages do they bring us?

Angels convey good news and bad news. They announce the birth of special children. They bring God's call to those chosen for special missions. They both warn and reassure people who face dangerous situations. They bring the bad news of God's judgment and sometimes administer the punishment for wrongdoing. They also interpret visions that are too difficult for the human recipients to understand.

15. Who are the special persons in the Bible whose birth is announced by angels?

The first person whose birth is announced by an angel is Abraham's son Ishmael (Gen 16:7–12). His mother Hagar has fled into the desert because Sarah, her mistress, was treating her harshly. The angel tells her that she is pregnant with a son, instructs her to name him Ishmael, and gives her a glimpse into the child's future. Another announcement comes centuries later, when the Israelites are being oppressed by the Philistines. An angel of the Lord appears to the wife of Manoah to tell her that she will conceive and bear a son; the angel also instructs her to raise the child as a nazirite, vowed to God, and tells her that her son will deliver Israel from the Philistines (Judg 13:2–5). When the wife of Manoah reports this to her husband, he wants to hear the message with his own ears. So the angel returns and repeats the message for her husband (Judg 13:6–23). Their son is Samson.

16. Do angels announce the birth of any special persons in the New Testament?

In Luke's Gospel the angel Gabriel announces to Zechariah that his wife Elizabeth will conceive and bear a son, and he tells the parent what to name the child: John. He also instructs Zechariah to raise his child as a nazirite, and describes the child's future. When Zechariah cannot believe this good news because he and his wife are old, the angel gives him a sign: he will be mute until the child is born (Luke 1:5–23). The same angel announces to Mary, betrothed to Joseph, that she will have a son. The angel tells her to name the child Jesus and reveals the child's wonderful future. When Mary questions the angel, he gives her a sign too: the pregnancy of her cousin Elizabeth (Luke 1:26–38).

17. Doesn't Scripture also tell us that God sometimes uses angels to call people to do special tasks?

God does indeed use angels to ask people to do special and difficult things. The story of Moses' call begins when an angel of the Lord appears to him in a burning bush (Exod 3:2). After the angel gets Moses' attention, the Lord commissions him to deliver the people from Egyptian oppression. The appearance of the angel to Moses is recalled in New Testament times, in Stephen's speech before the Sanhedrin (Acts 7:30, 35). In the time of the Judges, when Israel is being oppressed by the Midianites, an angel of the Lord appears to Gideon and greets him, "the Lord is with you" (Judg 6:12). Gideon objects that the Lord doesn't seem to be with him at all but seems to have abandoned the people to their enemies. The Lord commissions Gideon to take care of this desperate situation by delivering Israel from the hand of Midian (Judg 6:13–19). Then when Gideon offers this messenger bread and meat, the angel touches the food with his staff, sets it aflame, and then disappears. Gideon realizes that this was an angel speaking to him. He cries out to the Lord in fear and the Lord reassures him (Judg 6:20–23). In both these stories the identities of the angel of the Lord and the Lord are blurred. It seems that Moses and Gideon *see* the *angel* of the Lord but actually *hear* the *Lord*. Later I will say more about the "angel of the Lord" (see questions 29–31).

In the New Testament, too, angels are sent to call people to do a special task. The angel of the Lord sends the apostle Philip to go down to the Gaza road to meet a court official of the Ethiopian queen. Philip overhears the Ethiopian eunuch reading a passage from Isaiah and uses that passage to tell him the good news about Christ. The eunuch is led to faith by Philip's words and, when they spy some water, Philip baptizes the eunuch. Then Philip, having accomplished his task, is snatched away to Azotus (Acts 8:26–40). In a later story in the Acts of the Apostles, an angel instructs the Roman centurion Cornelius to summon Peter (Acts 10:3–7). When Peter asks the messengers why they have come, they reply: "Cornelius, a centurion, an upright and God-fearing man, who is well spoken of by the whole Jewish nation, was directed by a holy angel to send for you to come to his house and to hear what you have to say" (Acts 10:22). Peter goes to the house of Cornelius, tells him the story of Jesus, and, when the Holy Spirit comes upon them all, Peter baptizes them, the first Gentile converts to Christianity (Acts 10:23–48).

18. Do we really have guardian angels?

Yes, both Scripture and tradition assure us of the comforting truth that we each have a guardian angel. The foundation of the church's teaching on guardian angels is Jesus' warning to the disciples not to despise even little children because "in heaven their angels continually see the face of my Father in heaven" (Matt 18:10). In his commentary on this passage, St. Jerome observed: "how great the dignity of the soul, since each one has from birth an angel commissioned to guard it." The tradition of guardian angels is found in the Acts of the Apostles too. When the maid Rhoda announced that Peter, who had just been rescued from prison by an angel, was knocking on the door, the people inside who were praying for him said, "It is his angel" (Acts 12:15). Then Rhoda, perhaps thinking that an angel could come through any obstacle, didn't even open the door, so Peter had to keep on knocking!

This New Testament tradition of guardian angels has an Old Testament foundation. Several angels guard and guide individuals. Angels lead Lot out of burning Sodom (Gen 19:15–22). When Abraham's servant raises objections about finding a bride for Isaac, Abraham reassures him that God will send an angel to show him the way (Gen 24:7, 40). In his blessing of Ephraim and Manasseh, Jacob mentions an angel who has redeemed him from all harm (Gen 48:16). The archangel Raphael protects young Tobiah from a dangerous fish and a jealous demon (Tobit 5—12). Psalm 91 declares that God commands the angels to guard us in all our ways (Ps 91:11–12) and Psalm 34 promises that "the angel of the Lord encamps around those who fear him and delivers them" (Ps 34:7).

When Nebuchadnezzar had the three young men thrown into the fiery furnace because they would not worship the statue, "the angel of the Lord came down into the furnace to be with Azariah and his companions, and drove the fiery flame out of the furnace, and made the inside of the furnace as though a moist wind were whistling through it" (Dan 3:26–27 [3:49–50 Greek]). Nebuchadnezzar, when he discovers their rescue, exclaims, "Blessed be the God of Shadrach, Meshach, and Abednego, who has sent his angel and delivered his servants who trusted in him" (Dan 3:28). When Daniel escapes unharmed from the lion's den, where he was thrown for praying against the king's order, he reports to the king: "My God sent his angel and shut the lions' mouths so that they would not hurt me, because I was found blameless before him" (Dan 6:22 [6:23 Hebrew]). There is no clear indication, however, that any of these angels stayed with their charges throughout the person's lifetime, as we now believe guardian angels do.

St. Basil thought that angels guarded only believers: "An angel attends everyone who believes in the Lord if we never chase him away by our evil deeds" ("Homily 16: On Psalm 33[34]"). He says again, "Beside each believer stands an angel as protector and shepherd leading to life." But Thomas Aquinas states clearly that *every* human being has a guardian angel. St. Ambrose exhorts us to "pray to the angels who are given to us as guardians." Aquinas also teaches that our guardian angels remain with us even in heaven. That is a wonderful promise—that we will enjoy their company for all eternity!

19. Do angels guard only individuals or do they guard groups of people as well?

Besides guarding individuals, angels also guard whole communities of people. Angels are frequently described as leading and protecting the people Israel. At the exodus event, when the people are trapped with the sea in front of them and the Egyptian army behind them, "the angel of God who was going before the Israelite army moved and went behind them" to shield them from the Egyptians (Exod 14:19). As they journey through the wilderness, God promises: "I am going to send an angel in front of you, to guard you on the way and to bring you to the place that I have prepared" (Exod 23:20; see 23:23). God also warns them to pay attention to the angel and listen to him carefully. If they rebel against the angel, he will not forgive them, but if they obey him God will protect them against all enemies (Exod 23:21–22). After the people have broken the covenant by making the golden calf, God refuses to go any farther with them but offers to send an angel before them to drive out the inhabitants of Canaan (Exod 32:34; 33:2). Moses, however, convinces God to continue to journey with them (Exod 33:12–17). As they approach the land, Moses sends messengers to Edom and announces that God "sent an angel" to bring them out of Egypt (Num 20:16).

God also assigns angels to guard other nations and peoples. "When the Most High apportioned the nations, when he divided humankind, he fixed the boundaries of the peoples according to the number of the gods" (Deut 32:8; *angelos* in Greek). Churches too have guardian angels. The letters to the seven churches in the Book of Revelation are addressed to their angels (Rev 2:1, 8, 12, 18; 3:1, 7, 14), who are described as seven stars in the right hand of Christ (Rev 1:16, 20). Although some commentators have assumed that these angels are the bishops of the various churches, the consistent appearance of angels in the Book of Revelation suggests that this passage, too, really speaks of angels.

20. If angels protect us, do they also warn us ahead of time of impending danger? Are there any stories in the Bible of angels warning people and reassuring them of God's protection in the future?

Angels seem to be particularly active when human beings are in danger or distress. There are many stories of angels warning people and reassuring them that God will not abandon them. Angels warn Lot of the destruction about to come upon Sodom and instruct him to flee the city (Gen 19:15). When Hagar flees into the wilderness with her son Ishmael, an angel tells her not to be afraid and reassures her that God will make a great nation of her son (Gen 21:17–18). An angel stops the hand of Abraham when he is about to sacrifice his son Isaac (Gen 22:11–12). With the danger averted, the angel then introduces God's renewal of the covenant promise to Abraham (Gen 22:15–18). In the incident of Balaam and his talking donkey, an angel of the Lord is the messenger of God's anger. He warns the prophet to speak only what he is told by God to speak (Num 22:22–35). When the prophet Elijah is fleeing from the anger of Jezebel, an angel feeds him and strengthens him for the journey to Mount Horeb, where he will receive a message from God reassuring him that he will not die but has a future task to accomplish (1 Kgs 19:6–7).

21. What about the New Testament—does it have any stories of angels helping people out of dangerous situations?

Matthew's Gospel has several stories of an angel helping St. Joseph in difficult situations. When Joseph discovers that Mary, his betrothed, is pregnant, an angel of the Lord reassures him in a dream and instructs him to go ahead and take Mary as his wife. The angel also gives him the good news of the child's origin and future (Matt 1:20–24). When Herod decides to massacre the children of Bethlehem, an angel instructs Joseph in a dream to take his young family to Egypt (Matt 2:13–15). When the danger is past, the angel assures Joseph that he and the family can return to their land (Matt 2:19–21). Is it an angel who warns him in a fourth dream that the tyrant Archelaus is ruling over Judea, so that he decides to go to Nazareth of Galilee instead of back to Bethlehem (Matt 2:22–23)? The previous stories certainly suggest that it is.

Angels help the apostles several times in the early days of preaching the Good News. The angel of the Lord rescues them when they are imprisoned by the high priest and his company and instructs them to "tell the people the whole message about this life" (Acts 5:17–20). Later, the detailed story of Peter's rescue from prison tells of an angel awakening him, instructing him to dress and follow, and then leading him past the guards and through the outer gate that opens of itself. Only when the angel leaves does Peter realize that this is not a vision but is really happening to him (Acts 12:6–11).

22. Where are angels leading us?

Tradition teaches that our guardian angels guide us always toward God. They encourage us to choose good actions instead of evil ones and to act according to our human dignity. Their only power is through encouragement; they cannot force us to do or think anything. But they are God's agents to help us through the difficulties of life. The archangel Raphael guided Tobiah on his journey and taught him how to capture the life-threatening fish and then use it to heal his father and his bride (Tobit 6). The angel God promised to the Israelites in the desert guided them toward the promised land (Exod 23:20). These examples assure us that our guardian angels are leading us in the right direction.

23. Do angels sometimes bring messages that are not so good? How are the angels messengers and ministers of judgment in the Bible?

In Psalm 35 the psalmist begs God to defeat his enemies: "Let them be like chaff before the wind, with the angel of the Lord driving them on. Let their way be dark and slippery, with the angel of the Lord pursuing them" (Ps 35:5–6). There are several specific examples of angels either announcing judgment or also executing it.

Toward the end of his life, David decides to take a census of the people, probably either for purposes of military draft or taxation. Later David realizes that this action was wrong and appeals to

God for forgiveness. God's answer comes through the prophet Gad, who offers David three choices: three years of famine, three months of enemy pursuit, or three days' pestilence. David chooses the pestilence (2 Sam 24:1–14). But when an angel is sent to destroy Jerusalem, the Lord relents and stops him (2 Sam 24:15–17). In the retelling of the story in 1 Chronicles 21, the angel of the Lord then commands the prophet Gad to tell David to erect an altar on the threshing floor of Ornan the Jebusite (1 Chr 21:18–19). The threshing floor becomes the site of the Jerusalem temple.

In the eighth century BCE, Sennacherib, ruler of Assyria, laid siege to Jerusalem. King Hezekiah of Judah prayed to God for deliverance and the Lord sent word to him through the prophet Isaiah that Sennacherib would not succeed. "That very night the angel of the Lord set out and struck down one hundred eighty-five thousand in the camp of the Assyrians" (2 Kgs 19:35; Isa 37:36).

When Jesus explains the parables about the final judgment to his disciples, he says that the reapers who separate the wheat from the weeds are the angels (Matt 13:39, 41). At the end of the age "the angels will come out and separate the evil from the righteous" (Matt 13:49). Jesus warns his followers to remain true to him, because, when he comes in glory with the angels, he will be ashamed of those who have been ashamed of him and will repay them for what they have done (Matt 16:27; Mark 8:38; Luke 9:26; 12:9). Another description of the day of judgment portrays the angels with Christ when he sits on his throne separating the sheep from the goats (Matt 25:31).

24. Is there really such a thing as an angel of death?

There are two opposing images for the "angel of death." Sometimes the "angel of death" is regarded as a frightening figure. This fear is related to the angels' task as messengers and ministers of judgment. Sometimes the "angel of death" is even equated with

Satan. On the other hand, the tradition of angels guiding us toward God has led to a belief that an angel will accompany us through the mystery of death. This angel will guide us on the final journey through the devastation of death to happiness with God. Some ancient manuscripts of the Gospel of Luke tell of an angel who came to strengthen Jesus before his death (Luke 22:43). In Jesus' parable about Lazarus and the rich man, the angels carry Lazarus to the bosom of Abraham (Luke 16:22). When the disciples ask Jesus what will happen at the "end of the age," Jesus tells them that the angels will gather all God's elect at the end of time (Matt 24:31).

25. Angels have interpreted some difficult and complicated visions. Can you talk about some of them?

Early prophets like Amos and Isaiah (eighth century BCE) seemed to understand their visions without an interpreter. But a later prophet, Zechariah (sixth century BCE), needed help. At the beginning of the book that bears his name, Zechariah has a series of seven visions: four horsemen (1:8-13), four horns and four blacksmiths (2:1–4; NRSV 1:18–21), a man with a measuring cord (2:5–9; NRSV 2:1–5), a lampstand flanked by olive trees (4:1–5, 11–14), a flying scroll (5:1–4), a woman in a basket (5:5–11), and four chariots (6:1–8). An angel is present with him and talks to him whenever he sees a vision. Zechariah keeps asking questions about the meaning of the visions (e.g., 1:9, 21; 4:4; 6:4) and sometimes the angel encourages him to inquire, saying, "What do you see?" (4:2[Heb 4:1]; 5:2; see 4:5, 13). Each time the angel explains the vision to him. The angel also speaks to other angels who are in the visions and to the Lord (1:10–13; 4:3–5).

In a later book (second century BCE) Daniel too has a hard time understanding his visions. As he is struggling to understand a vision of a ram and a goat, someone looking like a man appears and speaks to him. Daniel reports: "I heard a human voice by the Ulai, calling, 'Gabriel, help this man understand the vision'" (Dan 8:15–16). Then the angel explains, detail by detail, what the vision means (Dan 8:18–26). Even after this angelic clarification, Daniel says, "I was dismayed by the vision and did not understand it" (8:27). After this, Daniel ponders the seventy years that the prophet Jeremiah predicted for the devastation of Jerusalem (Dan 9:1–2; see Jer 25:11–12; 29:10) and prays for mercy and for insight (Dan 9:3–19). The "man" (angel) Gabriel comes to him again and says, "I have now come out to give you wisdom and understanding.... for you are greatly beloved" (9:20–23). Then Gabriel proceeds to explain the seventy years, which he calls "weeks" (9:24–27). In another vision, Daniel sees "a man clothed in linen" who promises "to help [him] understand what is to happen to [his] people at the end of days" (10:5, 10–14). Then another "one in human form" explains to him what is to happen in the future (10:18; 11:1–45). The angel reveals to him that the righteous will awake to everlasting life (12:1–3). This angelic message is the only direct promise of resurrection in the Hebrew Scriptures.

In the New Testament angels are very helpful to the visionary John in the Book of Revelation. First, an angel brings the revelation and its explanation (Rev 1:1). Then John sees the angels offering the prayers of the saints (8:3–5); he sees the consequences of their blowing the trumpets (8:6—9:21). He is told to eat the scroll from the angel's hand (10:8–11). The angels announce to him the destruction of Babylon (14:6–12) and show it to him (17:1–18). Finally, an angel shows him the new Jerusalem (21:9). He is told that God has "sent his angel to show his servants what must soon take place" (22:6; see 22:16). Angels have certainly shown this visionary many wonderful things!

26. Do angels have a special language?

Paul seems to indicate that angels have their own language when he says, "If I speak in the tongues [i.e., languages] of mortals and of angels..." (1 Cor 13:1). Two books belonging to the pseudepigrapha also speak of the angels' language. The Testament of Job describes the daughters of Job singing God's praise "in the angelic dialect" and "in accord with the hymnic style of the angels" (48–50). In the Apocalypse of Zephaniah, the prophet claims to know the language of the angels so that he can pray with them (8.4). But in their ministry as messengers, the angels communicate clearly to human beings. Thus they must be speaking a language the hearers understand. Usually angels seem to communicate through words, but sometimes angels begin their message only by appearing. For example, an angel summons Moses by appearing to him in a burning bush. An angel stops Balaam in his journey by appearing to his donkey with a drawn sword; only when Balaam has stopped does the angel deliver the message verbally. The angels in the Book of Revelation sometimes speak to John, but at other times they simply show him the vision.

27. Do angels know everything?

Angels are wise and they know more than human beings: they see the face of God and they are given privileged information to convey to people. But angels do not know everything. When Raphael is encouraging young Tobiah to marry Sarah, he comments: "I presume you will have children by her" (Tob 6:18). He presumes this future event, but he does not know for sure. Jesus describes to his disciples the events that will precede the future coming of the Son of Man, and then adds, "about that day or hour, no one knows, neither the angels in heaven, nor the Son, but only the Father" (Mark 13:32; par. Matt 24:36). The author of 1 Peter reminds his readers of the great gift they have received in the revelation of the good news in Christ. He declares that this revelation that has been announced to them is something even the angels did not know. These truths about Christ are "things into which angels long to look" (1 Pet 1:12).

28. You mentioned earlier that angels have power over the natural world. What does this mean?

Several biblical stories describe angels affecting various natural elements. In Jesus' time sick people came to the Pool of Bethesda because it was said that an angel of the Lord stirred up the water. Whoever got into the water first after this stirring was healed. Jesus himself healed a man who could never get to the water soon enough (John 5:1–9; see v. 4). The Book of Revelation's dramatic description of the end times shows angels in charge of all the elements: Four angels hold back the four winds so that they cannot blow (Rev 7:1); four angels are given power to damage earth and sea (Rev 7:2); an angel has authority over fire (Rev 14:18) and another over waters (Rev 16:5).

29. When the Bible speaks about the "angel of the Lord," is this really another name for God?

The title "angel of the Lord" is mysterious. Sometimes, particularly in the Pentateuch (the first five books of the Old Testament), the angel of the Lord seems to be another way of talking about God. When Hagar, pregnant with Abraham's child, runs away from Sarah, the angel of the Lord finds her in the wilderness and tells her to return to Sarah (Gen 16:7–9). But what the angel of the Lord says next suggests that it is really God speaking: "*I* will make your descendants so numerous that they will be too many to count" (Gen 16:10). Hagar certainly thinks so: "So she named the Lord who spoke to her, 'you are El-roi'" (that is, "the God of Vision"; Gen 16:13). A similar ambiguity arises when the angel of the Lord stops Abraham from sacrificing Isaac and then says, "now I know that you fear God, since you have not withheld your son, your only son, from *me*" (Gen 22:12). The angel of the Lord continues: "By *myself* I have sworn, says the Lord: Because you have done this, and have not withheld your son, your only son, I will indeed bless you" (Gen 22:16–17; see also Moses in Exod 3:1–6).

The same ambiguity appears in the humorous story of Balaam and his donkey. When Balaam, who has been summoned by the king of Moab to curse Israel, sets out with the princes of Moab, "God's anger was kindled because he was going, and the angel of the Lord took his stand in the road as his adversary" (Num 22:21–22). Three times the donkey sees the angel of the Lord and stops, but Balaam sees nothing. Finally, the third time the donkey talks to Balaam and he sees the angel of the Lord, who then speaks to him (Num 22:23–34). Then the angel of the Lord gives him permission to go, but warns him: "speak only what *I* tell you to speak" (Num 22:35). Isn't this God? Balaam later tells the king, "The word *God* puts in my mouth, that is what I must say" (Num 22:38). Is the angel of the Lord really the Lord?

An angel of the Lord appears to Joshua and the Israelites and announces, "*I* brought you up from Egypt, and brought you into the land that *I* had promised to your ancestors. I said, '*I* will never break my covenant with you'" (Judg 2:1). The people know who did these things. They know it's not just an angel; they offer sacrifice to the Lord (Judg 2:5; see also Gideon in Judg 6:11–16). Throughout the announcement to Manoah and his wife that they will have a son (Samson), the narrator reports that the angel of the Lord brings this message (Judg 13:3, 13, 15–18, 20–21). Manoah's wife tells her husband it was a "man of God," who looked like "an angel of God" (13:6; see 13:8, 10–11). When the angel of the Lord ascends in the fire of the sacrifice, "Manoah realized that it was the angel of the Lord," but he says to his wife, "We shall surely die, for we have seen *God*" (13:20–22).

30. But is the angel of the Lord sometimes distinct from God?

The previous passages suggest that the angel of the Lord is the Lord God. In other texts, however, the angel of the Lord seems to be separate from God. The Lord sends the angel of the Lord to destroy Jerusalem as punishment for David's census (2 Sam

24:15–16). In the later telling of the story in Chronicles, the angel of the Lord also commands the prophet Gad to tell David to build an altar on the threshing floor, the site of the future temple (1Chr 21:15–18). David worshiped there instead of at Gibeon because he was afraid of the sword of the angel of the Lord (1 Chr 21:30). When Jerusalem is besieged by Sennacherib, it is an angel of the Lord that strikes the Assyrian soldiers and forces the army to retreat (2 Kgs 19:35; 2 Chr 32:21; Isa 37:36).

The angel of the Lord sometimes visits prophets. Elijah is encouraged by the angel of the Lord, who feeds him on his flight from Jezebel; this food strengthens him for his journey to Mount Horeb where he will meet God (1 Kgs 19:7; see 19:5). The angel of the Lord also tells Elijah how to respond to King Ahaziah of Israel and when it is safe to meet the king (2 Kgs 1:3, 15). Zechariah, whose visions are explained to him by an angel, also sees the angel of the Lord, who appeals to God for the sake of Jerusalem (Zech 1:11–12) and for Joshua the high priest (Zech 3:1–10).

Psalm 34 assures righteous people that "the angel of the Lord encamps around those who fear him, and delivers them" (Ps 34:7; Heb 34:8). But, according to Psalm 35, the wicked should fear the pursuit of the angel of the Lord (Ps 35:5–6). The angel of the Lord goes into the fiery furnace with Azariah and his companions and protects them (Dan 3:49, see 3:95; NRSV 3:28). The young Daniel names the angel of the Lord as the one who will execute judgment against the accusers of Susanna (Dan 13:55, 59) and some Greek manuscripts describe that judgment: "The angel of the Lord threw fire in their midst and saved the blood of the blameless one on that day" (13:60–62; LXX). When Daniel himself is thrown into the lions' den, it is the angel of the Lord who snatches up Habakkuk and carries him to the lions' den to feed Daniel (Dan 14:31–39).

The Septuagint (the Greek translation of the Old Testament made between the third and first centuries BCE) reflects the later tendency to move away from describing the appearance of God directly, but to refer to the angel of the Lord instead. For example, where the Hebrew text says that "the Lord" attacked Moses to kill him, the Septuagint says that an angel of the Lord attacked him (Exod 4:24). The Septuagint removes the ambiguity regarding Gideon's call, naming the person who appears to him as the angel of the Lord throughout (see question 29 and Judg 6:14, 16).

31. Does the angel of the Lord appear in the New Testament as well?

Yes. In the New Testament the angel of the Lord brings messages from God but is clearly distinct from God. In the gospels the angel of the Lord appears in the context of important births (as in the Old Testament) and at the empty tomb after Jesus' resurrection. In the Gospel of Luke it is an angel of the Lord who announces to Zechariah the coming birth of John the Baptist (Luke 1:10–20). (This angel of the Lord is later identified as Gabriel who brings the news to Mary concerning Jesus' birth; Luke 1:26–27). The angel of the Lord, accompanied by a multitude of the heavenly host, announces Jesus' birth to the shepherds (Luke 2:8–15). In the Gospel of Matthew the angel of the Lord enlightens Joseph concerning Mary's pregnancy and instructs him to take her as his wife, which he does (Matt 1:20–24). The angel of the Lord also instructs Joseph to take Mary and Jesus to Egypt to avoid Herod's massacre and informs him when it is safe to return to Israel (Matt 2:13, 19–20). At the end of Matthew's Gospel the angel of the Lord comes down from heaven, rolls back the stone that sealed Jesus' tomb, and sits on it. His appearance paralyzes the guards stationed at the tomb and the angel informs the women of Jesus' resurrection and instructs them to go and tell the disciples (Matt 28:2–7).

In the Acts of the Apostles the angel of the Lord continues to fulfill the promise of Psalms 34 and 35, delivering those who fear God and pursuing the wicked (see Ps 34:7; 35:5–6). When the high priest has the apostles put in the public prison, "an angel of the Lord opened the prison doors, brought them out," and instructed them to continue their preaching about Jesus (Acts 5:17–20). Later when Herod plans to kill Peter, an angel of the Lord leads him out of prison, melting away his chains, blinding the guards, and opening the city gate (Acts 12:2–11). As for Herod, who considers himself equal to God, "an angel of the Lord struck him down, and he was eaten by worms and died" (Acts 12:21–23). The angel of the Lord also continues the mission of instructing the bearers of God's word, sending Philip to interpret Isaiah for an Ethiopian eunuch and to baptize him (Acts 8:26–38).

32. What is meant by the "choirs" of angels?

In Christian tradition the angels are organized into a hierarchy of nine ranks or "choirs": angels, archangels, virtues, powers, principalities, dominions, thrones, cherubim, and seraphim. "Angel" is the common generic biblical name; the titles "seraphim" and "cherubim" also appear in the Old Testament. The New Testament provides the title of "archangel" (1 Thess 4:16; Jude 9). "Principalities and powers" are named in the New Testament letters as spiritual creatures (Rom 8:38; Eph 3:10; Col 1:16), not always in a positive light (Eph 6:12; Col 2:15)! "Thrones and dominions" are added by Colossians (Col 1:16). St. Jerome uses some of these names to talk about angels as "thrones, dominations, powers, seraphim, cherubim" (Eph 1:21). But it is St. Gregory the Great, who died in 604, who gives us the traditional nine choirs as listed above, moving from least to greatest. Thomas Aquinas arranges these nine choirs into three groups of three, based on their nearness to God.

33. The seraphim sound rather awesome. What kind of angels are they?

The seraphim are the highest choir of angels. The word *seraph* in Hebrew means "burning." The seraphim are believed to be on fire with the love of God. When God calls Isaiah to be a prophet, Isaiah sees seraphim around God's throne. Their appearance seems similar to humans, with faces and feet, but they are also described with six wings: two cover their faces, two cover their bodies, and two keep them aloft (Isa 6:2). The seraphim sing God's praise: "Holy, holy, holy is the Lord of hosts; the whole earth is full of his glory!" (Isa 6:3). Overwhelmed by this vision, Isaiah cries out in recognition of his unworthiness, and one of the seraphim touches his lips with a coal from the altar fire to cleanse him (Isa 6:5–7).

The word *seraph* is also applied to serpents, perhaps because of their burning bite (see Num 21:6; Deut 8:15). The prophet Isaiah describes seraph serpents as flying (Isa 14:29; 30:6). For this reason, it has been suggested that the image of the seraphim is based on the flying cobra, called the uraeus, honored in ancient Egypt as a guardian of the Pharaoh and pictured on the Pharaoh's crown. Can you imagine flying cobras in Isaiah's vision?

The Israelites encounter seraph serpents in the wilderness when they rebel against God who sends these burning serpents among them. When Moses cries out for mercy, God instructs him to mount a seraph on a pole; anyone who looks at it is healed (Num 21:4–9). Later a bronze serpent called "Nehushtan" is placed in the temple to commemorate this healing. The Nehushtan may be what Isaiah saw at the beginning of his vision. During Isaiah's lifetime King Hezekiah had the Nehushtan destroyed because the Israelites were worshiping it as a god (2 Kgs 18:4). In the New Testament this uplifted seraph who heals the people becomes a symbol of the crucified Christ, the source of our life (John 3:14–15).

Seraphim appear outside the Bible too. St. Francis of Assisi received the stigmata, the wounds of Jesus in his body, in a vision of a seraph on the feast of the exaltation of the cross, September 14, 1224. Teresa of Avila also had a vision in which a seraph pierced her heart, revealing Christ's love for her and her sharing in his suffering.

34. What about the cherubim? Are they really the cute, childlike angels depicted in popular religious art?

Scripture does not depict them that way! They are awesome, powerful beings. The cherubim are named as the second rank of angels in the heavenly hierarchy. After God drives Adam and Eve out of the Garden of Eden, God assigns the cherubim along with "a sword flaming and turning to guard the way to the tree of life" (Gen 3:24). Cherubim appear most frequently, however, as the guardians of God's throne. A golden cherub stands on each side of the Ark of the Covenant and their wings stretch out over the Ark (see Exod 25:18–20; 37:7–9). In Solomon's temple these cherubim are large enough that one wing of each cherub touches the side wall of the Holy of Holies and their other wings meet over the Ark (1 Kgs 6:27). Their combined wingspread is said to be twenty cubits, that is, about thirty feet (2 Chr 3:11–13)! These cherubim are probably modeled on throne guardians in Assyria and Babylon, winged animals resembling lions or bulls. Representations of these figures have been found across the Middle East ranging from small ivory carvings in Samaria to huge statuary at the Assyrian capital of Nineveh. Images of them on friezes from Nineveh can still be seen in the British Museum.

Because the Ark of the Covenant was considered to be the throne of God, God is frequently called the one "enthroned upon the cherubim" (1 Sam 4:4; 2 Sam 6:2; 2 Kgs 19:15; Isa 37:16; Ps 80:2; 99:1; 1 Chr 13:6). God comes to the rescue of the faithful, riding or flying upon the cherubim (Ps 18:11; 2 Sam 22:11).

The four living creatures that Ezekiel sees in Babylon at the time of his call (Ezek 1:5–21) are later identified as cherubim (Ezek 10:15, 17). In a dramatic vision Ezekiel sees the Lord, enthroned on these cherubim, leaving the temple and the doomed city of Jerusalem and pausing on the Mount of Olives (Ezek 10:4, 18–19; 11:22–23). The Mount of Olives is only a temporary resting place, however; God's destination is Babylon. The presence of the cherubim and the vision of God's throne at the time of Ezekiel's call (Ezekiel 1) give powerful testimony to the truth that the Lord God is not confined within the Jerusalem temple but has even gone to Babylon with the exiled people.

35. We hear a lot about the archangels. Can you explain who they are?

The archangels are named in lists of either seven or four. In the Book of Tobit, Raphael says he is "one of the seven angels who enter and serve before the Glory of the Lord" (Tob 12:15). These seven angels who stand in God's presence appear again in the Book of Revelation (Rev 8:2). These seven angels are the "archangels." Of these seven, only Raphael, Gabriel, and Michael are named in the Bible. Tradition, especially in the apocrypha and pseudepigrapha, gives us the names of other archangels as Uriel (or Phanuel), Raguel, Sariel, and Remiel (see 1 Enoch 40.8–9). Sometimes only four archangels are named: the three biblical archangels and Uriel (Phanuel). These angels who stand before God are sometimes called the "angels of the presence."

36. Before the Vatican II liturgical reforms we used to pray after Mass, "St. Michael the archangel, defend us in battle." Can you say more about St. Michael?

The name of the archangel Michael means "Who is like God." Daniel is told that "Michael, the great prince" is the guardian of his people and will protect them from the great distress to come in the end times (Dan 12:1; see 10:13, 21). Michael is also the one who brings the good news of resurrection: "Many of those who sleep in the dust of the earth shall awake; some to everlasting life, and some to shame and everlasting contempt" (Dan 12:2). In the New Testament Michael appears as a powerful force at the end times, leading the angels who are victorious over the dragon, who wants to devour the child of the woman crowned with twelve stars (Rev 12:7–9). The Letter of Jude reports that, despite his great power, the archangel Michael did not dare to pronounce judgment against the devil but left judgment to God (Jude 9). In 1 Enoch he is called "the merciful and forbearing," and he is the one who describes the power of the tree of life whose fruit will be given to the righteous (1 Enoch 40.9; 25:1–7). All these events certainly inspire awe. Michael's name is appropriate: "Who indeed is like God!" (See question 54 about praying to angels.)

37. What about Gabriel? We see him in pictures of the annunciation, don't we?

Gabriel, whose name means "God is my strength," is sent by God to explain to Daniel his mysterious vision of a ram and a goat and their extraordinary horns (Dan 8:16–26). A second time Gabriel comes to give Daniel "wisdom and understanding" and to inform him that his prayer for his suffering people has been heard (Dan 9:22–27). In the New Testament Gabriel announces to Zechariah that his wife Elizabeth will give birth to a son whom he should name John. He is also sent to Mary to tell her that she will conceive and bear a son, Jesus (Luke 1:19, 26). When Enoch is taken up to the seventh heaven and left alone there, Gabriel comes to encourage him: "Be brave, Enoch! Don't be frightened! Stand up, and come with me and stand in front of the face of the Lord forever!" (2 Enoch 21.3). All four of these people—Daniel, Zechariah, Mary, and Enoch—need God's strength brought to them by this angel. (For more about pictures of the annunciation, see question 49.)

38. So Michael is a protector and Gabriel comes to strengthen people to hear God's word. What about Raphael?

Raphael, whose name means "God heals," exercises his healing ministry by teaching, guiding, and protecting, especially against demons. He is a teacher. He teaches Tobiah how to use the entrails of the fish to heal both his father's blindness and his wife's demonic possession (Tob 6:3–9, 17–18; 11:8). He is also a teacher of prayer and good works. He instructs both Tobit and Tobiah to be faithful to prayer, fasting, and especially almsgiving (Tob 12:8–9). Raphael is a guide. He leads Tobiah on his journey. In spite of Tobiah's intention to go to Rages in order to collect the money his father has deposited there, Raphael leads him to Ecbatana where he will find his wife (Tobit 6—8). He guides both Tobiah and Sarah back to the house of his father Tobit in Nineveh (Tobit 11). Meanwhile he goes to Rages to collect the money deposited long ago by Tobit (Tobit 9). He protects against demons. He pursues the demon Asmodeus to Egypt and binds him there so that he may no longer afflict Sarah (Tob 8:3). In 1 Enoch he is sent by God to "bind Azazel hand and foot and throw him into the darkness" (1 Enoch 10:4). He is also commissioned to "give life to the earth which the [fallen] angels have corrupted" (1 Enoch 10:7). Wherever Raphael goes, he brings good health.

39. I have heard of a fourth angel named Uriel, but I can't find him in the Bible. Who is Uriel?

Uriel, whose name means "light of God" or "fire of God," appears only in later Jewish books. In 1 Enoch he watches in horror, along with Michael and Gabriel, the violence and oppression occurring on the earth (1 Enoch 9.1). Fittingly, this angel of light is the guide of the heavenly luminaries, stars, moon, and sun (1 Enoch 72.1; 82.7–8). Uriel also informs Enoch of the fate of the fallen stars, the fallen angels (1 Enoch 21.5, 10). He is sent to teach Ezra of the impossibility of understanding the ways of God, but he also tells him the signs of the end of the world and instructs him to fast for seven days (4 Ezra 4—5). With Michael, Gabriel, and Raphael he is named as one of the "imperishable angels of immortal God" and is reported to know all about the final judgment (Sibylline Oracles 2.215).

40. Why do so many angelic names end in "el"?

El is the Hebrew word for God. The names of the angels indicate the tasks they were called to do. Each one comes representing a special characteristic of God that the angel is called to exercise on behalf of human beings.

41. Do angels tell us their names?

We do have names for some angels (see especially question 35 above), but in general angels are hesitant to reveal their names. When Manoah asks the name of the angel who came to announce the impending birth of Samson, the angel replies, "Why do you ask my name, which is mysterious?" (Judg 13:17–18). The "man" who wrestles with Jacob responds in similar fashion when Jacob asks his name: "Why should you want to know my name?" (Gen 32:29). Jacob identifies this stranger as God (Gen 32:31) but when the prophet Hosea retells the story, he is more cautious: "He [Jacob] strove with God; he strove with the angel and prevailed" (Hos 12:4–5). When Tobit wants to know the name and family of the "man" who will guide his son to Media, Raphael replies, "Why do you need to know my tribe?" Tobit insists on an answer and Raphael replies, "I am Azariah, the son of the great Hananiah, one of your relatives" (Tob 5:11–13).

42. Raphael doesn't seem very honest there. Do angels always tell the truth?

Raphael does not give his true name, but his name is nonetheless accurate. Azariah means "the Lord is my help," and Raphael has come to bring God's help to Tobit. He has also told Tobiah that he is an Israelite, a relative, who has come to work (Tob 5:5). It is true that he has come to work, but is he an Israelite and a relative? Certainly not in the way that Tobiah will understand those words.

The angelic reluctance to reveal too much to the human beings to whom they are sent may be a way of protecting people and preserving their freedom. If Tobiah had known Raphael was an angel, would he have been so quick to take responsibility for his own life as he does in the marriage negotiations? If Tobit had known Raphael's identity, would he have dared to exercise authority over him by sending him as guide with his son?

43. Are angels as great as God?

No, angels are creatures of God just as human beings are. They stand in God's presence and serve God, as Raphael says (Tob 12:15; see Heb 1:14). They are sent by God to human beings (see, for example, Gen 24:7, 40; Exod 23:20; 33:2; Num 20:16; Dan 3:95 [NRSV 3:28]). We call upon them to worship God with us (Ps 103:20; Dan 3:58; see Rev 7:11) but we are warned not to worship *them* (Col 2:18). When John, the visionary of the Book of Revelation, falls down "to worship at the feet of the angel" who reveals these things to him, the angel says to him, "You must not do that! I am a fellow servant with you.... Worship God!" (Rev 22:8–9; see Rev 19:10).

44. Are angels greater than Christ?

No. The Letter to the Hebrews says that Christ, the Son of God, is "as much superior to angels as the name he has inherited is more excellent than theirs" (Heb 1:4). The author of this letter uses Psalm 8 to testify that, for a little while, Jesus was made "lower than the angels," but now he is "crowned with glory and honor" and all things are subject to him (Heb 2:8–9; see Eph 1:20–22; Col 2:15). The angels *serve* Jesus on earth. They minister to him after the temptation in the wilderness (Matt 4:11; Mark 1:13) and at the agony in the garden. He is certain that the Father would send twelve legions of angels to defend him against those who come to arrest him (Matt 26:53). The angels are instructed by God to *worship* Christ who is God's firstborn (Heb 1:6). We are told that Christ sits "at the right hand of God, with angels, authorities, and powers made subject to him" (1 Pet 3:22). At the end of time the angels will gather faithful people and bring them to Christ who comes as judge (Matt 16:27; 24:31; 25:31; Mark 8:38; 13:27; Luke 9:26; 12:8–9)

45. Do angels have free will?

We believe that angels now enjoy the glorious vision of God in heaven. Thus they cannot sin; they can only do good. The stories of the fall of the angels, however, suggest that at one time they could make the choice between good and evil. In both Jewish and Muslim tradition the angels are said, surprisingly, to be inferior to human beings because human beings have free will, the power to choose good or evil, a power the angels no longer have.

46. Do angels ever feel sad?

According to St. Ambrose, a fourth-century doctor of the church, the angels grieve because they must administer penalties to those who sin. "They who enjoy the life of beatitude would surely prefer to return to that high state of peace rather than be involved in avenging the punishment of our sins," he writes. But he also says that they live in hope that we will share with them the joys of eternal glory. In a letter to St. Irenaeus he envisions the angels joining with us in building the heavenly temple. "We must not doubt that in the building of this temple the company of heavenly hosts will join with us, for it is unbecoming that human love can build up a temple of God, so that there is formed a dwelling of God in us, while this is not possible among the powers of heaven."

47. Can we see angels?

Angels are pure spirits; they do not have bodies. So with our bodily eyes, we cannot see them as they truly are. When angels are said to appear to people, therefore, they take on a different form. Usually they appear as human beings. Tobit and Tobiah see Raphael simply as a fellow Israelite (Tobit 5—6). But even if angels appear to be human beings, they have extraordinary characteristics. The angel who appears to Manoah and his wife rises up with the flame of the sacrifice they offer (Judg 13:20–21). Raphael ascends to heaven after delivering his final message to Tobit and Tobiah (Tob 12:21). Cornelius reports that the angel who appeared to him is clothed in dazzling robes (Acts 10:30; see Rev 10:1).

Sometimes the appearance of angels is not described but their power is felt. Daniel says that an angel closed the mouths of the animals in the lions' den (Dan 6:20–24); an angel gives instructions to the apostle Philip (Acts 8:26). But neither person says anything about what the angels look like. Their purpose is not to be seen themselves but to reveal God. St. Augustine says that "an angel is said to give understanding to a human being, just as a person could be said to give light to a house by making a window." The one who makes the window does not make the light, but only makes it possible for the light to shine in. Just so, "God made the angel into the kind of being who can bring about some change in the human mind to make it capable of admitting the divine light."

48. Then do angels really have wings and haloes?

Angels are often portrayed with an aura of light, which we call a "halo." Their clothes too are often described as shining and luminous. This light all around them signifies their closeness to God who is all light. Because they are in union with God and enjoy the vision of God, God's light shines through them. Wings are a way to indicate the swiftness and freedom of movement characteristic of angels. Since they are pure spirits, they can move with the speed of thought. Raphael, for example, makes it back and forth from Ecbatana to Rages in record time! It took Alexander the Great eleven days of forced march to cover the two hundred miles one way, but Raphael makes it there and back within the fourteen days of Tobiah's wedding celebration (Tob 9:2–6; see 8:20).

49. Many great artists have painted angels in different ways. Can you talk about some of those?

There have been some common artistic conventions throughout the centuries for portraying angels. Since around the fourth century CE, artists often portray angels with wings. These wings are usually white, but the Italian artist Fra Angelico (ca. 1395–1455), in his fresco of the annunciation (mid-fifteenth century), presents an angel with brightly colored wings and a brightly colored gown. In his painting of the annunciation (ca. 1503), the artist Raphael (1483–1520) (not the angel!) shows a dark-winged angel. The seventeenth-century Dutch artist Godfried Schalcken (1643–1706) omits the wings altogether and instead portrays Gabriel with clouds around his ankles and a light around his head. The angel in *Ecce Ancilla Domini* by the English artist Dante Gabriel Rossetti (1828–82) has no wings, but fire surrounds his feet. The clouds and fire also indicate that these angels are not part of the earthly realm and are not limited by earthly bodies.

Angels are often shown gowned in white, but in Leonardo da Vinci's (1452–1519) painting of the annunciation, the angel is finely dressed in colored drapery. A twentieth-century Korean artist, Woonbo Kim Ki-chang (1914–2001), portrays Gabriel in Korean dress with his wings like ribbons swirling all around and blending with a ribbon-like cloud beneath him.

Many artists envision angels with full bodies like adult human beings. The Spanish artist El Greco (1541–1614) paints strong masculine angels on either side of the *Virgin of the Immaculate Conception*. These brawny angels appear again in his *Assumption*, along with more childlike angels at Mary's feet. In Raphael's *Coronation of the Virgin*, the angels above Mary's head are little round faces surrounded by four wings, while those at her feet appear as winged toddlers. Beside Mary are full-figured adult angels playing musical instruments. The American artist Henry Ossawa Tanner's (1859–1937) painting *The Annunciation* portrays the angel as a pillar of light standing at the foot of Mary's bed and illuminating the whole picture.

The posture of angels differs in various artistic representations. Often they are standing, but Donatello (ca. 1386–1466) (in a stone carving with gilded highlights, ca. 1435) and Leonardo da Vinci portray Gabriel kneeling at the annunciation, while one of Fra Angelico's paintings of the annunciation shows the angel bowing to Mary and pointing toward her with one hand and upward with the other in one. In Raphael's *Annunciation* Gabriel is running into a pillared courtyard to greet Mary.

50. All those artists seem to portray angels with Jesus' mother, Mary. Do any artists portray the guardian angels or angels, with saints?

There are many popular as well as classic depictions of guardian angels. Many children grew up with a picture over their beds of a guardian angel leading a little child across a bridge.

The American artist Thomas Cole (1801–48), in a series called *The Voyage of Life*, depicts four periods of a man's life: childhood, youth, manhood, and old age. A guardian angel appears in each of the four paintings. In the first painting, *Childhood*, the guardian angel, a young winged man dressed in white with a large radiating halo around his head, is guiding a boat on a river with the child seated in front of him. The figurehead of the boat is also an angel holding an hourglass, symbolizing the passing of time. The angel is the brightest part of the painting.

In the second painting, *Youth*, the angel stands on shore gesturing with his hand palm up, allowing the young man in the boat to set his own direction. In the third painting, *Manhood*, a much darker, stormier scene, the angel at first glance seems to be absent, but upon closer inspection one finds his faint figure far away, behind and above the man in a break in the clouds. The dark clouds threaten and take the shape of evil spirits. In the final painting, *Old Age*, the angel is again in the boat, right in front of the white-bearded man who sits calmly in the boat. The figurehead with the hourglass is broken off; time has run out. The angel points the way toward the end of the journey—a large bright opening in the clouds through which other angels seem to be riding beams of light down toward the two figures in the boat.

Cole's sensitive portrayal of the guardian angel shows the angel present throughout the person's lifetime, but most obviously so at the two most vulnerable periods of life: childhood and old age. During youth and maturity the angel seems to allow the person more freedom and space.

In his illustrations for Alfred Lord Tennyson's poem "The Palace of Art" (1857), Rossetti shows St. Cecilia with her hands on the organ keyboard and the angel not only looking at her, as described in the poem, but kissing her. She leans her head back and closes her eyes to meet his kiss. The angel, minus wings and a halo, is dressed in a rich cloak and carries a banner.

51. How do angels figure in classic poetry and drama?

In the *Divine Comedy*, Dante Alighieri (ca. 1265–1321) describes the choirs of angels as concentric circles whirling around the pure light of God. The seraphim and cherubim are the innermost circles, whirling with the greatest speed and burning with the most intensity. The rest of the choirs move more slowly and burn less brightly, depending on their distance from God. William Shakespeare (1564–1616), in *Macbeth*, notes both the glory and the fall of the angels: "Angels are bright still, though the brightest fell." Hamlet, at the appearance of the ghost of his father, calls upon the angels to defend him. The final lines of *Hamlet* echo the liturgical chant *In Paradisum* (see question 53): "Good night sweet prince, and flights of angels sing thee to thy rest." John Donne, a contemporary of Shakespeare, calls for the angels to blow their trumpets at the last judgment and raise the dead.

In *Paradise Lost* (1667) John Milton describes the archangels' involvement in the events surrounding creation. The archangel Gabriel, alerted to an evil presence by the archangel Uriel, drives Satan out of Eden after his first and unsuccessful effort to tempt Eve. The archangel Raphael, "the sociable spirit," tells Adam of the fall of the rebel angels into hell. Raphael explains the creation of human beings and warns Adam not to eat the forbidden fruit and not to seek knowledge that is beyond him. The archangel Michael, who has driven Satan and the fallen angels out of heaven (see question 65), is also sent to expel Adam and Eve from Eden. He brings a comforting message, however; he promises Adam that a messiah will come to redeem them.

The nineteenth-century poet Lord Byron describes the angel of the Lord as an angel of death in his poem "The Destruction of Sennacherib" (cf. 2 Kings 19:35–36).

52. What do more contemporary writers have to say about angels?

Angels figure in the German poet Rainer Maria Rilke's (1875–1926) cycle *Das Marienleben* ("The Life of Mary"). In "The Annunciation" it is not the angel Gabriel's appearance that startles Mary, but the deep communication between them as their eyes meet. In "Joseph's Suspicion," which describes the angelic appearance to Joseph, Joseph is angry and murmuring, but the angel cries out to him to understand God's work in Mary as he understands God's work in the wood he handles every day. When Joseph grasps the mystery, the angel disappears. "Of the Death of Mary," which alludes to Mary's assumption into heaven, imagines Gabriel coming once more to take Mary to heaven. Again she is startled, but relaxes as the angel summons the disciples.

Two contemporary novelists are inspired by the Book of Tobit. In Andrew Greeley's *Angel Light* (1995), the archangel Raphael is disguised as an extraordinary female travel agent who turns out also to be a healer and a matchmaker, while Frederick Buechner, in *On the Road with the Archangel* (1997), lets Raphael serve as the narrator who makes witty observations from the angelic point of view about the characters and the action.

53. Don't we hear a lot about angels in our music too? What do the hymns and carols tell us about the angels?

The Gregorian chant *In Paradisum*, which is often sung as the body is taken from the church at the end of a funeral, alludes to the angels' role as our guardians: "May the angels take you into paradise; may the martyrs come to welcome you on your way and bring you into the holy city Jerusalem." The fourth-century hymn "Of the Father's Love Begotten" (*Corde natus ex Parentis*) calls upon the angel hosts to adore the newborn Christ: "Powers, dominions, bow before him, and extol our God and King, " while another ancient chant related to the birth of Christ, the Marian antiphon *Alma Redemptoris Mater*, composed in the eleventh century and sung at the end of night prayer during Advent, appropriately recalls the greeting of the archangel Gabriel to Mary: "Virgin before and after that Ave that came from the mouth of Gabriel,"

In more recent times the Anglican clergyman Sabine Baring Gould (1834–1924) made a popular translation of an annunciation carol from the Basque. "The Angel Gabriel from Heaven Came" gives a haunting description of Gabriel at the annunciation: "His wings as drifted snow, his eyes as flame."

Not unexpectedly, many songs in which angels figure prominently are connected with the incarnation and are thus sung at Christmas. Many popular carols sing of the angels' annunciation to the shepherds ("Hark! The Herald Angels Sing," "Angels We Have Heard on High"); in others the angels join the earthly realm in praising the newborn king ("Angels, from the Realms of Glory," "O Come, All Ye Faithful!"). Several classical composers have used the juxtaposition of high and low voices to telling effect to suggest a dialogue between heaven and earth. They include Handel (1685–1759), in his *Messiah* ("Glory to God in the highest"), and Palestrina (ca. 1524–94), in the motet for eight voices, "*Hodie Christus natus est*" ("Today Christ is born").

Other familiar hymns that call upon the angels to praise God include "Let All Mortal Flesh Keep Silence," "Praise the Lord! You Heavens, Adore Him," and "Ye Watchers and Ye Holy Ones." In our singing we are very aware that the angels bring us messages from God and join us in praising God. Perhaps nowhere else are we so conscious of our closeness as fellow creatures of God.

54. Can we pray to angels?

We can pray to angels in the same way that we can pray to saints, as fellow creatures of God who want to help us on the way. A document from Vatican Council II, *Lumen Gentium* (1964), commends the veneration of the saints, "together with the Blessed Virgin Mary and the holy angels," and asserts that the "Church has piously implored the aid of their intercession" (*Lumen Gentium* ¶ 50). We do not, however, worship angels. Worship is given to God alone.

A traditional prayer to our guardian angel is:

Angel of God, my guardian dear,
To whom God's love commits me here,
Ever this day be at my side,
To light and guard, to rule and guide.

A prayer for protection against the forces of evil in the world, addressed to the archangel Michael, was introduced by Pope Leo XIII in 1886 and ordered to be recited after all Low Masses (Masses that were not sung):

> St. Michael, the archangel, defend us in battle. Be our protection against the malice and snares of the devil. May God rebuke him, we humbly pray; and do thou, O prince of the heavenly host, by the power of God, thrust into hell Satan and all evil spirits who prowl about the world seeking the ruin of souls.

These prayers after Mass were suppressed in 1964 with the reforms of Vatican II.

We also commemorate Gabriel's announcement to Mary when we pray the *Angelus* and we use his words in the first part of the "Hail Mary" (Luke 1:28).

55. Are there only "popular" prayers to the angels? Or do we call on the angels in our liturgy as well?

We call upon the angels to join us in prayer several times in liturgical worship. At Eucharist the joyful song "Glory to God in the Highest" begins with the song of the angels who announced Jesus' birth to the shepherds (Luke 2:14). At the end of the preface to the eucharistic prayer the presider invites us to sing with the angels again: "So, with all the choirs of angels in heaven we proclaim your glory and join in their unending hymn of praise" (Eucharistic Prayer I). We respond with the song of the seraphim who appeared when Isaiah was called to be a prophet: "Holy, holy, holy is the Lord God of hosts. All the earth is filled with his glory" (Isa 6:3). The psalms in the Liturgy of the Hours often invite the angels to pray with us: for example, "Bless the Lord all you angels" (Ps 103:20–21); "Praise God, all you angels; give praise, all you hosts (Ps 148:2).

56. Have any of the great saints outside of the Bible seen angels?

A well-known story concerns St. Augustine (354–430), bishop of Hippo and one of the great doctors of the church. Once when Augustine was walking by the seashore at Civitavecchia and struggling to understand the doctrine of the Holy Trinity, he saw a young boy pouring seawater into a hole in the sand. He asked the boy what he was doing, and the boy replied that he was attempting to pour the whole sea into this hole. Augustine laughed and said, "That is impossible." "Just so," said the boy, "is your attempt to contain the whole mystery of the Trinity in your small human mind." This story became a favorite subject for art and stained glass windows.

Thus it is not surprising that St. Augustine later told the story of an angel who had a lesson to teach. A certain Gennadius doubted whether there was any life after death. A handsome youth appeared to Gennadius in his dreams and led him to a city where he heard extraordinarily sweet singing. The next night the same youth appeared and asked if Gennadius recognized him. When Gennadius answered yes, the youth reminded Gennadius that he had seen him in a dream and was again seeing him in a dream. By asking how he saw him, even though he was asleep, he led Gennadius to understand that we see things, not only with our physical eyes, but also in dreams. So the body is not the whole of life. Thus Gennadius came to believe in the resurrection. The youth who instructs Gennadius is, as St. Augustine says, an angel.

When St. John Bosco (1815–88), the founder of the Salesians, was ministering to the poor, he was often threatened by robbers. A large black dog began accompanying him through the dangerous places. When John arrived at a place of safety, the dog would vanish. As with Augustine and the boy at the seashore, angels may appear in various disguises!

57. Do we become angels when we die?

No; if we have believed in God and lived according to God's law, we become saints. Our faith teaches us that we will rise from the dead, body and soul. When Jesus rose from the dead, he consistently showed his apostles that he was not a ghost (that is, a spirit without a body), but that he had a glorified body as well. He ate with them (Luke 24:42–43), walked with them (Luke 24:15), and allowed them to touch him (Matt 28:9; Luke 24:39–40). His body is transformed: he can move with great speed (compare Luke 24:13, 29-31, 33–34), go through doors and walls (John 20:19), and ascend to heaven (Luke 24:51). But Jesus in heaven still has a human body. We also believe that Mary, his mother, was assumed into heaven body and soul. These examples help us to believe that we too will enjoy heaven as whole human beings, in contrast to the angels, who are pure spirits and have never had bodies.

PART TWO

Devils or Fallen Angels

58. Who or what is Satan?

In the Old Testament *satan* is usually not a proper name; the satan is an adversary or opponent. In Psalm 109 the psalmist begs God to find an accuser (a satan; Ps 109:6) to accuse his opponent in a law court. After quoting all the accusations that the opponent has made against the psalmist, he prays that all these evils might come instead on his accusers (satans; Ps 109:20; see also 109:4, 29; Ps 38:21; 71:3). Sometimes the satan is a military enemy. When David fled from Saul and was fighting with the Philistine army, the Philistine chiefs forbade him to enter into a battle with the Israelites, because they were afraid he would become their opponent (satan) and join with his own people (2 Sam 29:4; see also 1 Kgs 5:18). Sometimes the satan is a political enemy. Two men who attempt to rebel against Solomon, Hadad and Rezon, are identified as satans (1 Kgs 11:14, 23, 25). The adversary may appear as a friend who tempts a person to do something rash. Abishai attempts to convince David to execute Shimei, who cursed him, but David declares that no one will die for participating in the rebellion against him. David calls Abishai a satan (2 Sam 19:23). Not all these opponents are human. Even the angel of the Lord who stops Balaam and frightens his donkey is acting as a satan to hinder him (Num 22:22, 32).

In later texts the satan is identified as one of the members of God's heavenly court, one of the sons of God, thus one of the angels. This heavenly being convinces God to afflict Job in order to test his fidelity (Job 1:6–9, 12; 2:1–4, 6–7). The prophet Zechariah has a vision in which the high priest Joshua is standing before the angel of the Lord. Satan stands at his right hand to accuse him while the angel of the Lord defends him (Zech 3:1–2; see Ps 109:6).

59. How do the Gospels depict Satan?

In the Gospels Satan is a proper name for the personification of evil, the tempter. Jesus is tempted by Satan in the desert (Mark 1:13) and drives him away: "Get away, Satan!" (Matt 4:10). When Jesus is accused of driving out demons by the prince of demons, he challenges his accusers: "How can Satan drive out Satan?" (Mark 3:23) and observes that if Satan is divided against himself, he cannot stand (Mark 3:26; Matt 12:26; Luke 11:18). Satan is the one who steals the word of God out of human hearts (Mark 4:15). The Gospel of Luke is much clearer in attributing to Satan the source of all the evil that afflicts humankind. In Luke Jesus says that the bent-over woman has been bound by Satan for eighteen years (Luke 13:16). When the seventy-two disciples return from their mission of preaching and healing, Jesus praises them for driving out the power of evil and says, "I saw Satan fall like lightning from the sky" (Luke 10:18). Jesus warns Peter that Satan will tempt him, but he also encourages him: "Satan has demanded to sift all of you like wheat, but I have prayed that your own faith may not fail; and you, when once you have turned back, strengthen your brothers" (Luke 22:31–32). Luke and John observe that Satan entered into Judas. Luke says Satan's entrance tempted Judas to betray Jesus to the chief priests; John sees Satan entering Judas at the supper after Jesus identifies him as the betrayer (Luke 22:3; John 13:27).

In at least one gospel passage, however, the term *satan* seems to be a tempter or adversary in the sense of the Old Testament word. When Peter objects to Jesus' statement that he will suffer and die, Jesus says to him, "Get behind me, Satan! You are an obstacle to me" (Matt 16:23; see Mark 8:33).

60. Is Satan the same as the devil?

The idea of Satan as personified evil, equivalent to the devil, is a late development in ancient Israel. The Greek Septuagint shows this development. In earlier books such as the story of Balaam in Numbers, the translators recognized the meaning of satan as "adversary" (Num 22:22, 32; see 1 Sam 29:4; 19:23; 1Kgs 5:18; 11:14, 23, 25). But in later biblical books the translators regularly rendered Satan as *diabolos*, "devil" (1 Chr 21:1; Ps 109:6; Job 1:6–7, 9, 12; 2:1–4, 6–7; Zech 3:1–2). In the Gospels the names Satan and the devil are interchangeable. In the story of Jesus' temptation, for example, Mark reports that Jesus was tempted by Satan (Mark 1:13) while both Matthew and Luke say he was tempted by the devil (Matt 4:1, 5, 8, 11; Luke 4:2–3, 6, 13). Even in Matthew, however, Jesus refers to the tempter as Satan (Matt 4:10), and the one who induces Judas to betray Jesus in the Gospel of John is the devil (John 13:2). The one who takes the seed of God's word from human hearts is called the devil in the parable of the sower in Luke (8:12) and the evil one in Matthew (13:19). The ills that afflict human beings are said to be caused by the devil in Acts; in the Gospel of Luke they were caused by Satan (Acts 10:38; Luke 13:16).

The devil and his angels are in eternal fire, where wicked human beings will also be sent (Matt 25:41). Jesus calls his adversaries children of the devil who act according to the devil's wishes; he identifies the devil as a liar and the father of lies (John 8:44). In Acts it is Satan who tempts Ananias to deceive Peter and the apostles and keep profits for himself (Acts 5:3), but Paul calls Elymas, the magician who opposes him, a son of the devil (Acts 13:8–9).

The word devil, however, is also interpreted on at least one occasion as an accuser or opponent, just as the word satan is, and not as the spiritual personification of all evil. Jesus says to the disciples, "one of you is a devil," meaning Judas (John 6:70).

61. Did God create Satan?

Satan is indeed one of the creatures of God. God created everything that exists. God created Satan, like the other angels, to be full of goodness. But these spiritual beings were created like us with free will. So Satan chose to turn away from God and then became full of evil by his own choice. The Fourth Lateran Council declared, "The devil and the other demons were indeed created naturally good by God, but they became evil by their own doing" (see *Catechism of the Catholic Church* 391).

62. Then how did Satan, the devil, get to be so evil?

One of the stories of Satan's fall is told in the apocryphal work the Life of Adam and Eve (see question 8). According to this work, Satan was one of God's angels, created on the first day of creation. When God created human beings, the angels were told to fall down and do homage to Adam, created in God's image. So the archangel Michael worships God first and then pays homage to Adam. But when Michael summons Satan to do the same, he refuses, saying, "I was created before him; I will not worship him." For this reason Satan and his followers were cast out of heaven. His main goal since then has been the temptation of human beings, so that they too will be banished from heaven.

Origen, the third-century Christian theologian, tells another story of the fall of Satan. He begins by arguing that God did not create anything bad or wicked in the beginning, so Satan must originally have been good. He then takes Ezekiel's condemnation of the prince of Tyre (Ezekiel 28) and interprets it as a condemnation of Satan. The prince of Tyre is described in such glowing terms that Origen cannot believe this is a human being; rather, he must be a heavenly creature. He was "stamped with the seal of perfection, of complete wisdom and perfect beauty," and covered with precious jewels (Ezek 28:12–13). But pride corrupted this marvelous creature. He said, "I am a god" (Ezek 28:2). Therefore he was driven out of paradise and made a horror to all who see him (Ezek 28:15–19). Origen says that this passage refers to an adverse power who was formerly holy and happy. But "it fell from this state of happiness from the time that iniquity was found in it, and was hurled to the earth." He believes that these words are spoken of a certain angel. Origen identifies this angel as Satan or the devil.

63. Is Satan an "evil god"?

No, Satan is not an evil god. It is tempting to think of God as the supreme power of good and Satan as the supreme power of evil, but in no way is Satan equal to God. Even though we see so much evil in the world and feel incapable of overcoming it, God is still in charge. Satan is a creature of God, who, according to tradition, chose to turn against God.

When Jesus is tempted by Satan, the devil, he sends him off and refuses to listen to him. Later, when Jesus is accused of casting out demons by the power of Satan, he replies that if the accusation is true, Satan must be fighting against himself and his kingdom has come to an end (Luke 11:18). Jesus says, "But if it is by the finger of God that I cast out the demons, then the kingdom of God has come to you" (Luke 11:20). Jesus' miracles are a sign that God's kingdom has already arrived; there is nothing to fear. When Jesus commissions his disciples to heal, he tells them to announce this good news, saying to those who have been cured: "The kingdom of God has come near" (Luke 10:11). When the disciples return from their missionary journey, joyful at their success, Jesus says, "I watched Satan fall from heaven like a flash of lightning" (Luke 10:18).

The kingdom of God is present with us too. When we are tempted, we can call upon Jesus to help us refuse to listen to Satan. Satan cannot overpower God, nor can Satan overpower us if we rely on the strength of God within us. We don't need magic or superstitious practices to resist Satan. Satan has power over us, his fellow creatures, only if we surrender to him.

64. Who are the fallen angels? Are they Satan's companions?

A different tradition about the fallen angels develops from the mysterious passage in Genesis 6:1–4. The Genesis story says that the "sons of God saw that [human women] were fair" and "took wives for themselves of all that they chose." First Enoch says that this story is about the fall of the angels. ("Sons of God" is often interpreted as angels by those who translated the Hebrew Scriptures into Greek.) According to First Enoch, two hundred angels swore an oath that all of them would take human women as wives. The women subsequently gave birth to giants who ate all the available food, and so all creatures, even the earth itself, cried out against them. Michael, Gabriel, and another angel named Surafel watched the violence brought about by these giants and carried the plea of the people to God. God then warned Noah that a great flood was coming to expel these lustful angels and their children and to purify the earth. Enoch pleads with God for these angels, but God refuses to hear him. They are cast down into a "chaotic and terrible place," "the prison house of the angels who are detained there forever" (1 Enoch 6–15, 21).

65. I thought the rebellious angels were defeated in a war with the faithful angels. Is that true?

The story of the battle in heaven is yet another way of telling the story of the fall of Satan and his angels from heaven to earth and then to the netherworld. The Book of Revelation describes a battle in heaven after the great dragon (Satan) attempted to kill the child of the woman clothed with the sun. God snatched up the child and protected the woman in the desert. "Michael and his angels fought against the dragon. The dragon and his angels fought back, but they were defeated, and there was no longer any place for them in heaven. The great dragon was thrown down, that ancient serpent, who is called the Devil and Satan, the deceiver of the whole world—he was thrown down to the earth, and his angels were thrown down with him" (Rev 12:7–9). The Letter to the Ephesians suggests that this battle continues. Christians are warned to put on the armor of God in order to do battle against any temptation. "For our struggle is not against enemies of blood and flesh, but against the rulers, against the authorities, against the cosmic powers of this present darkness, against the spiritual forces of evil in the heavenly places" (Eph 6:11–12; see also Col 2:15; Rom 8:38).

66. Is the serpent in the Garden of Eden really Satan, the devil?

In Genesis 3, the serpent may be "more crafty than any other wild animal that the Lord God had made," clever enough to speak and carry on a conversation, but in this story the serpent is only an animal, one of God's creatures (Gen 3:1). God's judgment on the serpent shows it is simply a representative of all its kind: "upon your belly you shall go, and dust you shall eat all the days of your life" (Gen 3:14). Admittedly, however, this is an extraordinary serpent! It is able to talk and carry on a conversation; it is even able to convince Eve to eat the fruit. Why is this serpent so special? In the mythology underlying the story, the serpent may represent some foreign god, perhaps a god of wisdom. Nonetheless, the author of the story and the original audience could not have equated the serpent with Satan, since there was not yet a concept of an evil being who was the very personification of evil.

The earliest biblical identification of the serpent in the Garden of Eden as the devil is found in the Book of Wisdom, written in the mid-first century BCE. "God created us for incorruption, and made us in the image of his own eternity, but through the *devil's* envy death entered the world, and those who belong to his company experience it" (Wis 2:23–24).

About a century later, the Life of Adam and Eve presented the serpent as the mouthpiece of the devil. In this book Eve reports to her children: "Listen, all my children and my children's children, and I will tell you how our enemy deceived us." She tells how the devil had enlisted the serpent to do his dirty work, saying, "Do not fear; only become my vessel, and I will speak a word through your mouth by which you will be able to deceive him." The devil, speaking through the serpent, then carried on a conversation with Eve, first convincing her to eat the fruit and then persuading her to give it to Adam.

67. Talk about the "devil in disguise"! Satan, the devil, seems to go by many names. Can you mention some more?

Beginning in New Testament times, Satan is called by several other names. At the temptation of Jesus he is once called tempter (Matt 4:3). Paul also calls him that, worrying that the tempter had lured the Thessalonians away from the faith he had taught them (1 Thess 3:5). Sometimes Satan is also called the evil one. Jesus says it is the evil one who tempts us to make false oaths (Matt 5:37), who snatches away the word of God from the human heart (Matt 13:19), and whose children are the weeds in the wheat (Matt 13:38). Cain, the first murderer, is said to belong to the evil one (1 John 3:12); the whole world is under his power (1 John 5:19). In Matthew's version of the Lord's Prayer, we ask to be delivered from the evil one (Matt 6:13), and at the Last Supper Jesus prays for us, asking that his disciples be protected from the evil one (John 17:15). Faith is the shield against the evil one (Eph 6:16) and we have confidence that God protects us from him (2 Thess 3:3; 1 John 5:18; see 1 John 2:13–14).

In Matthew and Luke, Satan is occasionally called the enemy. The enemy sows weeds in the wheat (Matt 13:25, 28, 39). Jesus gives the seventy-two disciples the "authority to tread on snakes and scorpions, and over all the power of the enemy" (Luke 10:19). In the Gospel of John, Satan is also called the ruler of this world. Jesus announces that this ruler is coming (John 14:30), but he is already condemned (John 16:11) and will be driven out (John 12:31). Finally, in Revelation Satan is called the "dragon, that ancient serpent," recalling the story of temptation in Genesis 3 (Rev 20:2).

68. Satan also seems to have some "proper names." Can you explain some of them, like Beelzebul and Beliar?

Beelzebul is another name given to Satan in the New Testament. It is based on two Hebrew words: *Baal*, the name of a

Canaanite god, which means "lord" or "owner," and *zebul*, meaning either "prince" or "house." So Beelzebul is the owner of the house or the lord of princes. In the Old Testament this name refers to another god and is deliberately misspelled as Beelzebub, a derogatory term that means "lord of the flies" (2 Kgs 1:2–3, 6, 16).

This name, correctly spelled, is used in the Gospels as another name for Satan. Jesus says he has been called Beelzebul (Matt 10:25); he is accused of driving out demons by the power of Beelzebul (Matt 12:24, 27; Mark 3:22; Luke 11:15, 18–19). The name is explained in the gospels as "prince of demons" (Matt 12:24; Mark 3:22; Luke 11:15). But when St. Jerome translated the New Testament into Latin, he used Beelzebub instead of Beelzebul. So that spelling came into English translations and is much more familiar to Christians than Beelzebul.

Satan is called Beliar once in the New Testament. Paul asks, "What partnership is there between righteousness and lawlessness? Or what fellowship is there between light and darkness? What agreement does Christ have with Beliar?" (2 Cor 6:14–15). The name appears in the Old Testament as Belial, meaning "worthless," "wicked," or "good for nothing." Several times wicked people are called children of Belial (*bene-beliya'al*; see, e.g., Deut 13:13–16; Judg 19:22; 20:13; 1 Sam 2:12). The transition from calling such people children of Belial to identifying them as children of the devil in the New Testament seems a natural progression (see Acts 13:10; 1 John 3:10). Belial as a name for Satan also occurs in the Dead Sea Scrolls and in several works of pseudepigraphal literature.

69. Don't we sometimes hear the devil referred to as Lucifer?

Yes. When Isaiah denounces the king of Babylon, he calls him the morning star (Isa 14:12). Eventually Isaiah's condemnation of the Babylonian king was thought to be a description of the fall of Satan. It's not hard to see why. Isaiah says, "How you are fallen from heaven, O Day Star, son of Dawn! How you are cut down to the ground, you who laid the nations low! You said in your heart, 'I will ascend to heaven; I will raise my throne above the stars of God; I will sit on the mount of assembly on the heights of Zaphon; I will ascend to the tops of the clouds, I will make myself like the Most High.' But you are brought down to Sheol, to the depths of the Pit" (Isa 14:12–15).

So how did we get to Lucifer from this passage? When St. Jerome translated it into Latin, he used Lucifer (light-bearer) for morning star. So Lucifer became another name for Satan.

70. What threat is Satan, the devil, to Christians?

Christians are warned to watch out for Satan, who can even masquerade as an angel of light (2 Cor 11:14). His aim is to destroy them: "Like a roaring lion your adversary the devil prowls around, looking for someone to devour." God's faithful are to "resist him, steadfast in ...faith," confident that they are in union with believers throughout the world who are suffering the same afflictions (1 Pet 5:8–9).

More warnings appear throughout the New Testament. Satan's methods will take advantage of human weakness: exploiting human pride (1Tim 3:6), enmity between people (2 Cor 2:10–11), or even the hunger that comes from overzealous asceticism (1 Cor 7:5). The faithful are not to make room for the devil by nursing anger, but rather live as a new creation in Christ, forgiving one another (Eph 4:20–32, esp. 27). They are promised that if they resist the devil, he will flee. They must draw near to God, who will in turn draw near to them and give them the grace to be victorious (James 4:6–8).

Christians must always be on their guard, because Satan continues to afflict the faithful. The devil is seen as the cause of their suffering and imprisonment (Rev 2:10). Because of Satan, Paul's desire to visit the Thessalonians is thwarted (1 Thess 2:18). At other times Satan's affliction can be seen as a way to turn erring people back to the right path. Paul reports that he was disciplined by a messenger of Satan, to keep him from being too elated because of the revelations he had received (2 Cor 12:7). He also declares that wrongdoers should be handed over to Satan for discipline (1Cor 5:5; 1Tim 1:20). It can happen that people deliberately choose to surrender to Satan's power. "Everyone who commits sin is a child of the devil" (1 John 3:8–10; see 1 Tim 5:15). The seer of Revelation even calls a rival synagogue the synagogue of Satan (Rev 2:9; 3:9).

Christians, however, have a strong defender against Satan. The good news is that Christ has defeated him and saved us from his power. Christ, who shares our flesh and blood, was even willing to die, "so that through death he might destroy the one who has the power of death, that is, the devil, and free those who all their lives were held in slavery by the fear of death" (Heb 2:14–15). Paul advises us to "be wise in what is good and guileless in what is evil" and promises that "the God of peace will shortly crush Satan under [our] feet" (Rom 16:19–20). We are to "put on the whole armor of God, so that [we] may stand against the wiles of the devil" (Eph 6:11). We are to be gentle and kind to our opponents, hoping that God will lead them to repentance and truth "and that they may escape from the snare of the devil, having been held captive by him to do his will" (2 Tim 2:25–26). The victory has already been won; we must trust in Christ who has thoroughly defeated the powers of evil.

71. Satan is a really frightening figure in the Book of Revelation. Can you say more about this?

The Book of Revelation envisions the end of time as a great cosmic battle between superhuman powers of good and evil. Revelation 12 describes Satan as a great red dragon who threatens the woman about to give birth (Mary or the church giving birth to the messiah). The child is snatched up to heaven and the woman saved from the dragon-serpent. The dragon fights against Michael and the angels but is defeated by them. The dragon, identified as the ancient serpent of the Garden of Eden, the devil, and Satan, the deceiver of the whole world, is thrown down to earth with his angels, that is, the other spiritual beings that serve him; he eventually takes up a position on the sand of the sea. Unable to capture the woman, Satan, the accuser, wages war against her offspring, those who keep the commandments of God and hold the testimony of Jesus. They defeat him by accepting even death in order to give witness to Christ the Lamb.

As the end of time draws near in the visions of Revelation, chapter 20 describes how an angel chains Satan and throws him into a great abyss, which he locks and seals so that he cannot lead people astray for a thousand years. This thousand years is where the notion of the millennium comes from. After the millennium, or thousand years, Satan will be released for a short time to lead the nations into warfare. Then Satan, the devil, will be thrown into a pool of fire and sulfur where he will suffer forever.

72. What is Satanism?

Satanism is the term applied to the worship of Satan. It is essentially an antiChristian movement and in some cases also atheistic, that is, there is no belief in God. A ritual sometimes associated with satanism is the black Mass, a parody of the Catholic celebration of Eucharist. For "holidays" the Satanist movement has adopted what were legitimate folk celebrations with roots in Europe's pagan past. One of those is Halloween, when evil spirits are believed to be active, and the other is Walpurgisnacht (Walburga's Night), the evening before the feast of St. Walburga. In Goethe's story of Faust, a witches' sabbath takes place on Walpurgisnacht. This celebration occurs at the beginning of spring (May 1) and was thus traditionally a time for lighting bonfires to welcome the returning light—in some parts of northern Europe this is still done, simply as a surviving folk custom with no religious overtones—but our pagan ancestors never intended it as an occasion for satanic worship.

PART THREE

Demons

73. Who or what are demons?

Demons are evil spirits that afflict human beings with various ills. The Greek word *daimon* or *daimonion*, from which our English word demon comes, means some sort of divine being. In the ancient world a *daimon* could be either a good spirit or an evil one. In the biblical tradition demons are almost always thought to bring evil and to be dangerous.

The understanding of what devils or demons are and how they act is even broader and less clear in Scripture than the understanding of angels. In the earlier books of Scripture the gods of the other nations are sometimes understood as demons, or sometimes these foreign people are themselves demonized. In both the Old and New Testaments people afflicted with diseases are thought to be possessed by demons. Demons may also be the ghosts of people who have died. The apocalyptic worldview, which arose around the second century BCE, presents a clearer view of demons as superhuman malevolent spiritual beings.

74. The demons in the Old Testament are rather fearful. Who are they and what do they do?

The Old Testament tradition concerning demons reflects a fear of the unknown: of the desert wilderness, of strangers, and of death. Two kinds of demons are specifically named as inhabitants of the desert: satyrs or goat-demons (Hebrew *sa'ir*) and night-demons (Hebrew *lilith*). Isaiah, in his condemnationof Babylon, says that it shall become a wilderness populated by wildcats, owls, ostriches, and jackals. Goat-demons will dance there (Isa 13:21). He speaks the same curse over Edom: "From generation to generation it shall lie waste; no one shall pass through it forever and ever" (Isa 34:10). It shall be inhabited only by hawks, hedgehogs, owls, ravens, jackals, ostriches, wildcats, hyenas, and buzzards (Isa 34:11–15). There "goat-demons shall call to each other; there too lilith [a night-demon or screech owl] shall repose, and find a place to rest" (Isa 34:14; see Baruch 4:35 and question 86). In the chronicler's history, Jeroboam, the first king of Israel (the ten tribes in the north), is accused of placing not only golden calves at the shrines of Bethel and Dan but also goat-demons (2 Chr 11:15).

Foreign gods were also considered demonic. In both Deuteronomy and Psalm 106 the Israelites are accused of sacrificing their children to demons (Hebrew *shedim*). Deuteronomy observes that these demons are "not God" or "no-gods" (Deut 32:17; see Baruch 4:7). Psalm 106 identifies them as "the idols of Canaan" (Ps 106:37–38). The god to whom they are sacrificing is probably Molech, the god who claimed the firstborn. Leviticus forbids sacrificing children to Molech (Lev 18:21; 20:2–5), but the temptation to imitate the Canaanites seems to have persisted through the generations. Solomon built a high place for Molech, along with other foreign gods, in order to please his wives (1 Kgs 11:7); almost three centuries later Manasseh is condemned for the same action (2 Chr 33:6). In the early sixth century one of the reasons God is handing Jerusalem over to the Babylonians, according to Jeremiah, is because they are sacrificing their children to Molech (Jer 32:35). This abomination is happening in spite of Josiah's recent reform in which he destroyed the place where the sacrifices were taking place (2 Kgs 23:10). The Book of Isaiah condemns those who offer sacrifices to the gods called Fortune and Destiny (Isa 65:11); in the Septuagint these gods' names are translated simply as *daimon*.

75. What about the people in the Gospels who were said to be possessed by a demon?

In the Gospels Jesus encounters many such people. Some of these people are suffering from either physical or mental illness. Since the causes of these maladies were unknown to the people of Jesus' time, they thought that demons afflicted the sufferers. Some of these people were blind (Matt 12:22); some were deaf or mute

(Matt 9:32–33; Luke 11:14). Some seem to suffer from epilepsy (Luke 4:33–35; 9:42). Others are apparently afflicted with mental illness (Matt 8:28; Luke 8:27–30). Even actions that simply seem odd are attributed to demons. Because John the Baptist comes "neither eating nor drinking," people say, "He is possessed by a demon" (Matt 11:18; Luke 7:33).

76. So does Jesus drive out demons just as he sent Satan away?

Jesus does indeed drive out demons. This is part of his healing mission and one of his major works in the Gospels. His very first healing miracle in the Gospel of Mark is the cure of someone afflicted by a demon. The demon says, "What have you to do with us, Jesus of Nazareth? Have you come to destroy us? I know who you are, the Holy One of God." Then Jesus commands him to be silent and to come out of the man (Mark 1:23–27; Luke 33–37).

One of the most dramatic stories of Jesus expelling demons is the story of a man who was afflicted by so many demons that their name was Legion, indicating there were thousands of them (Mark 5:1–9). After Jesus commands the spirits to come out of the suffering man, they plead with Jesus to let them enter a herd of pigs nearby rather than driving them out of the territory altogether. Jesus agrees, and what follows indicates how many there were. About two thousand pigs plunged over the bank into the sea (Mark 5:11–13; see also Matt 8:28–34; Luke 8:27–39).

77. It seems that Jesus just speaks to demons and they come out of people. Does he use other methods too?

Jesus' commanding word is enough to drive out demons again and again (see Matt 8:16, 32; 17:18; Mark 5:8; Luke 4:35; 8:29). His command is powerful even at a distance. A foreign woman (identified as Syro-Phoenician in Matthew and Canaanite in Mark) begs him to drive a demon out of her daughter, who is lying sick at home (Matt 15:2–28; Mark 7:25–30). Although Jesus is initially reluctant to help her because he is convinced that his mission is to the house of Israel, he is persuaded by her wit. He commands the distant demon to leave the daughter, and at that moment the young woman is freed from her affliction.

But Jesus says that it is not only his word that is powerful against the demons but that prayer, too, is necessary. His disciples attempt to cast out a demon who is throwing a boy into convulsions, but they are unsuccessful (Mark 9:15–29; see Matt 17:14–18; Luke 9:37–42). The father then turns to Jesus, who has just arrived, and Jesus casts out the demon. The disciples want to know why. Jesus says, "This kind can come out only through prayer" (Mark 9:28–29).

Jesus always emphasizes the fact that demons are cast out by the power of God. When his opponents accuse him of casting out demons by the power of Beelzebul, prince of demons, he responds that he casts out demons by the "finger of God" (Luke 11:20) or the Spirit of God (Matt 12:22–28; see question 68). His work of driving out demons is a sign that the kingdom of God has entered into human history and the "strangle hold of personified evil" has once and for all been broken.

78. Do Jesus' disciples sometimes cast out demons too?

When Jesus sends his twelve disciples out on a missionary journey, he gives them authority not only to proclaim the kingdom of God and heal the sick but also to cast out demons (Luke 9:1–2; see Matt 10:1; Mark 3:15; 6:7). The Gospel of Luke reports that he later sent out the seventy-two disciples also (Luke 10:1–12). When they return from their journey, they are delighted with their success. They declare, "Lord, in your name even the demons submit to us!" (Luke 10:17; see Mark 6:13). After the resurrection the disciples continue their healing ministry, including the healing of those who are afflicted by demons (Acts 5:16; 8:7).

Initially the disciples are jealous of this power. They are unhappy when they find other people attempting to cast out demons in Jesus' name and succeeding (Mark 9:38; Luke 9:49; see Matt 7:22)! They complain about this to Jesus and report that they attempted to stop these people who were using Jesus' power but are not his disciples. Jesus, however, warns them not to stop anyone who is doing good in his name: "Whoever is not against us is for us" (Mark 9:38–40; Luke 9:49–50).

79. What happens to people when Jesus drives out the demons that afflict them?

Often the demons are thought to be what is making people sick. When the demon is expelled, the sick person is healed and returns to a normal life. For example, people bring a man to Jesus who is both blind and mute because of the power of a demon. Jesus casts out the demon and the man is able both to speak and to see (Matt 12:22). On another occasion a mute man speaks after Jesus casts the demon out of him (Matt 9:32–33; Luke 11:14). The neighbors of a man who was delivered from a "legion" of demons are astonished to see him sitting with Jesus, clothed and in his right mind (Mark 5:15; Luke 8:35). This story reveals a more significant result, however. This man who has been healed wants to follow Jesus. We are amazed that Jesus tells him no! Jesus has another job for him. He gives him a special commission: "Go home to your friends, and tell them how much the Lord has done for you, and what mercy he has shown you" (Mark 5:18–20; see Luke 8:38–40). So this former demoniac becomes a preacher of the good news!

80. Did Jesus really descend into hell, the haunt of demons, the way the Apostles' Creed says?

The phrase in the Apostles' Creed, "he descended into hell," means that Jesus really died and went to the place of the dead. In the Old Testament that place was called Sheol. Sheol was not a place of punishment, as we ordinarily think of hell today, but neither was it a place of joy. It can almost be imagined as a place of waiting under the earth where everyone went at death. Throughout most of the Old Testament period there was no belief in real life after death. The dead did not totally cease to exist, but they went to this place of suspended animation. In the Old Testament understanding of Sheol, there is neither pain nor delight, no memory, no communication, no light and warmth. The best thing that can be said for the situation of those in Sheol is that it is not nonexistence! Only when belief in life after death begins to emerge does the idea of Sheol turn into hell, a place of punishment for the wicked.

When we say that Jesus descended into hell, we mean that he went to Sheol, the place where all the dead were assembled. His presence there brings life-giving redemption to all good people who are in Sheol, those whose names we know, such as Abraham and David, as well as those who remain nameless. They will now share in the power of Jesus' resurrection and will join him in the joys of heaven. The story of Jesus' descent into hell or Sheol (Hades) is not told in Scripture but it does appear in an apocryphal gospel from the third or fourth century called the Gospel of Nicodemus. In this work, Joseph of Arimathea describes Jesus' arrival at the realm of the dead, his capture and binding of Satan, and the release of those imprisoned by him, beginning with Adam. (Note: By this time Sheol has indeed become hell, a dark, fearful place ruled by Satan.)

The statement in the creed that Jesus descended into hell, and especially the descriptions in the Gospel of Nicodemus, gave rise to a rich artistic tradition in the Middle Ages called the Harrowing of Hell. In some of these images Jesus is seen pulling people from the mouth of a monster, presumably Satan. Sometimes, as in John of Berry's *Petites Heures* (fourteenth century), hell is imaged as a castle spouting fire and surrounded by demons. In an ancient Cappadocian fresco, Jesus is standing on the devil and drawing people up out of the earth. In a woodcut by Albrecht Dürer the opening of the cave in the earth (Sheol) is an archway and light is beginning to break in. A fourteenth-century painting by Duccio di Buoninsegna (ca. 1255/60–1319) shows Jesus holding a cruciform standard with a banner flying. Some of those being released are identifiable, including an ancient, bearded Adam and David wearing a crown. Dürer and the Austrian Friedrich Pacher (1435-1508) also include Eve in the gathering of those being released. A fourteenth-century fresco in the Church of St. Francis in Assisi (presumably now damaged) shows Christ again pulling people out of a doorway built into a rock. Giotto painted a similar image. In most images Christ is drawing Adam up, and hell (Sheol) is a massive building with its foundations and building stones now cracked.

81. Jesus seems to have the demons under control. Do they bother Christians after Jesus' resurrection?

Christians are still threatened by forces of evil. We may not always call them demons, but we are still threatened by disease, violence, and our own lack of faith and of moral strength. As the Letter of James warns us, the wisdom that is characterized by "bitter envy and selfish ambition" is not from God but rather "is earthly, unspiritual, devilish" (James 3:14–15). Whatever works against love of God and love of one another is evil and can thus be considered "devilish" or demonic. Even the attempt to be holy by our own power without relying on God is not really holy but is selfish ambition. The author of First Timothy warns his readers that taking on rigorous ascetical practices, such as depriving ourselves of the food or sleep necessary to maintain health, is not only wrong but is deceitful and demonic (1 Tim 4:1–5). Such extreme practices deny the goodness of God's creation and do not build up the body of Christ. Their underlying purpose is to make ourselves look good and to win the admiration of others.

In the New Testament too the gods of other peoples are also regarded as demons. Paul warns Christians not to eat food sacrificed to idols, because these sacrifices are offered to demons, not to

God. He does not want the Corinthians to become participants with demons. He declares: "You cannot drink the cup of the Lord and the cup of demons. You cannot partake of the table of the Lord and the table of demons" (1 Cor 10:20–21). The worship of strange gods in the twenty-first century is more subtle and perhaps more dangerous. Money, comfort, fame can become the gods that we worship. These gods also demand sacrifices and offerings: addictions, violent seizure of what belongs to others, workaholism. Whatever threatens the integrity of human life lived in gratitude to God and compassion toward others can be demonic.

82. Are there choirs of demons like the choirs of angels?

A hierarchy of demons like the choirs of angels is not clearly represented in the tradition. But Dante, in the *Inferno*, does organize the demons in his nine circles of hell. Particular demons are associated with major sins, primarily the seven capital sins. The demons of lust are in the second circle (the first circle in Dante's *Inferno* is limbo, so there are no demons there), the demons of gluttony in the third circle, and of greed in the fourth. The fifth circle houses the demons of anger and sloth, the "noonday devil." In the sixth circle are the demons of heresy, not listed as one of the capital sins. The seventh circle is the haunt of the demons of violence and the eighth the home of the demons of fraud and theft. The ninth and final circle is reserved for the demons of treachery, with Lucifer, the most treacherous of all, at the center.

83. I keep hearing about the noonday devil. Just who is this?

The psalmist who wrote Psalm 91 lists a whole roster of dangers that the faithful need not fear because God will rescue them: the snare of the fowler, the destroying plague, the terror of the night, the arrow in the daytime (Ps 91:3–5). In verse 6 the terrors are "the pestilence that stalks in darkness" and "the destruction that wastes at noonday" (Ps 91:6). The Septuagint translated the Hebrew word for destruction or plague (*qeteb*) with the Greek word *daimonion*, "demon." The same word came into the Latin Vulgate, *daemonio*. So, Psalm 91 gave us the term, the "noonday devil."

In the Christian tradition the noonday devil became the experience of weariness in doing good, a kind of boredom with virtue. The energy of the beginning, the first fervor, is spent and the end is not yet in sight. Particular attention was paid to it regarding monks. A person would set out with great energy to embrace monastic life, but after several years the daily routine of prayer and work became so tedious that it seemed impossible to bear. The monastic term for this noonday devil was *accidie*, a Latin word meaning "having no care." In other words, the person afflicted by *accidie* does not care about anything but suffers from a kind of apathy. The fourth-century writer Evagrius has this to say: "the demon of *accedie*, also called the noonday demon, is the one that causes the most serious trouble of all."

Those burdened by *accidie* are tempted to flee the noonday devil with all sorts of distractions and busyness. But this flurry of activity leads to even more weariness. In his Rule, Saint Benedict does not use the term *accidie*, but he describes this temptation to overactivity in two kinds of monks who are afflicted by the noonday devil. The sarabites do not submit to the discipline of community life, but "their law is what they like to do, whatever strikes their fancy. Anything they believe in and choose, they call holy; anything they dislike, they consider forbidden" (*Rule of Benedict* 1.8–9). The "gyrovagues spend their entire lives drifting from region to region.... Always on the move, they never settle down, and are slaves to their own wills and gross appetites" (*RB* 1.10–11). But, as both Evagrius and John Cassian, another fourth-century monastic writer, say, the best antidote to this noonday devil is to stay put! Benedict praises the cenobites, those who live a faithful life within the community (*RB* 1.13). Or as a wise twentieth-century monastic woman once said, "Be where you are and do what you are doing."

The noonday devil does not afflict only monks, however. It is an all too common experience for people to become bored with marriage and to long for more excitement. People committed to prayer and the sacramental life can come to a point where participating in one more church service can seem utterly impossible. The monastic advice is still valid. Instead of fleeing our responsibilities, we must turn to them with even more energy. The cure for the noonday devil is discipline: the discipline of our thoughts, turning resolutely away from all the negative self-talk that fuels our apathy; and the discipline of our actions, being where we are supposed to be and doing what we are supposed to be doing—day after day. Finally, no demon is banished, as Jesus says, without prayer. Throughout our gritty perseverance we beg Jesus to restore to us a quiet, peaceful, happy heart.

84. The evil eye—what is that? Is it a demon?

The evil eye is not a specific demon but a quality that makes human beings demonic. In many cultures people who are thought to have the ability to cast the evil eye are greatly feared and various amulets are worn to protect people from their evil power. Even the Jewish Talmud, compiled between 200 and 500 CE, recommends wearing a little scroll of the priestly blessing from Numbers 6:24–26 around one's neck as a protection against the evil eye.

In the Bible the evil eye is the sin of envy. The envious person sees the prosperity of others and strikes them with the evil eye. In Jesus' story about the laborers in the vineyard, those who worked the whole day are envious of those who worked only an hour and received the same pay. The vineyard owner asks them: "Is your eye evil [i.e., envious] because I am generous?" (Matt 20:15). So in Jesus' list of the evils that come from the human heart, the evil eye is often translated as "envy" (see Mark 7:22). But while those who have too little are prone to envy, there is a corresponding affliction in those who have much. What they have is never enough, so the evil eye in them is greed and miserliness. The law warns the people not to be greedy (to have an evil eye) in their actions toward the poor in the sabbatical year when they are supposed to forgive all debts (Deut 15:9). If they are stingy and neglect to do this, God will hear the cry of the poor and punish the greedy. Tobit gives a similar warning to his son Tobiah: "Give alms from your possessions and do not let your eye begrudge the gift when you make it" (Tob 4:7, 16).

The Book of Proverbs even warns against eating with an evil-eyed person; his stinginess will make the food indigestible (Prov 23:6–8). Such people are so greedy that they are stingy with themselves, not only refusing to give to their neighbors but also neglecting themselves (Sir 14:8–10). This effect of the evil eye is described as devouring one's own flesh. When the people are attacked and besieged by their enemies, even the most refined among them will devour their own children and will have an evil eye against their surviving loved ones, snatching even this horrible food away from them (Deut 28:54–56). The evil eye is truly demonic!

St. Basil, a fourth-century doctor of the church, wrote a homily against the evil eye of envy and greed. He declares that demons use this evil eye for their own purposes. He warns that envy, not only of someone's wealth, but even of the wisdom and virtues of others, is demonic. The cure for this is to become honorable ourselves: doing good, acting with justice, enduring with patience. The acquisition of noble virtue is Basil's defense against the evil eye.

85. You mentioned that ghosts might be considered demons. Is that true?

The spirits of the dead (Hebrew *repha'im*) are sometimes considered demonic in the Old Testament. Their name, *repha'im*, may originally have been the name of a god of healing. But in the Bible they are inhabitants of Sheol (Isa 14:9, 26:14), a place where God's wonderful works cannot reach (Ps 88:10). (Remember that the belief in meaningful life after death did not arise in Israel until the mid-second century BCE; all the dead went to Sheol, a place similar to limbo in the Christian imagination.) In the Book of Proverbs two extraordinary women invite passersby to dinner (Prov 9:1–6, 13-18). But those who hear their call must be careful which invitation they accept. The unwary who accept the invitation of the woman folly instead of the woman wisdom end up in the company of the *repha'im* (Prov 9:18; see 2:18). Later in Proverbs we are warned, "Whoever wanders from the way of understanding will rest in the assembly of the dead" (*repha'im*; Prov 21:16). The spirits of the dead are to be avoided. Calling them up is everywhere forbidden (Lev 19:31; 20:6, 27; Deut 18:11; Isa 8:19). Saul, who had himself banned this practice, goes to a medium at Endor when he is in desperate straits. She is successful in summoning the spirit of Samuel for him (1 Samuel 28). Samuel brings no good news, however, but announces Saul's imminent death. The chronicler condemns Saul for seeking out a medium (1 Chr 10:13). The message is clear. Seeking information from the spirits of the dead instead of praying to God is always dangerous.

86. Are there other names for the evil forces that plague us?

There are a few other names in scripture for evil forces, such as Leviathan, Asmodeus, and Azazel, as well as some common words that become names for demons in later tradition, such as Lilith; Abaddon, the destroyer; and Mastema. All of these represent different kinds of evil.

Leviathan is the name of a great sea monster in the Old Testament; he is sometimes called a dragon. The ancient Near Eastern myths of creation described a battle between the god of the storm and the god of the sea. The storm god wins the battle and is able to confine the sea. Thus dry land appears and the creation of plants, animals, and humans is made possible. The sea becomes the symbol of chaos, whatever threatens to undo creation. Echoes of this myth appear in Genesis 1, but in the biblical story the one God who has power over all things confines the sea by a word and creates living beings. Other biblical references to creation, however, describe an encounter between God and Leviathan, the sea monster. In Psalm 74 God crushes Leviathan on the day of creation and feeds him to other creatures (Ps 74:13–15). The prophet Isaiah promises that, on the day of new creation, the day of the Lord, God will defeat Leviathan again: "On that day the Lord...will punish Leviathan the fleeing serpent, Leviathan the twisting serpent, and he will kill the dragon that is in the sea" (Isa 27:1). God the creator even plays with Leviathan, the symbol of chaos (Job 40:25—41:26; Ps 104:26).

In contrast to Leviathan, Asmodeus appears in only one Old Testament story. He is the demon in the story of Tobit who afflicts Sarah by killing seven of her bridegrooms on the wedding night. (Tob 3:8). The angel Raphael teaches Tobit's son Tobiah how to drive the demon away through prayer and terrible odors (Tob 6:8, 17). Raphael then pursues Asmodeus to Egypt and binds him there hand and foot (Tob 8:3). The evil that Asmodeus symbolizes is shown in his name, which is derived from the Persian words meaning "demon of wrath." He is a demon of wrathful jealousy.

The evil of death and destruction is also personified by spiritual beings. Are these demons or angels? They are sent by God, but those who suffer at their hands see them as evil. One such spiritual being is called the destroyer. In the tenth plague in Egypt, God sends the destroyer to strike down anyone who does not have the blood of the lamb on the doorpost (Exod 12:23; see Ps 78:49; 1 Cor 10:10; Heb 11:28). God also sends the destroyer to threaten Jerusalem with a plague in punishment for David's census (2 Sam 24:16). Another name for a spiritual being who brings death is Abaddon (Ps 88:12; Job 26:6; 28:22; 31:12; Prov 15:11; Rev 9:11). His name is based on the Hebrew word that means "destroy" or "perish."

Another demonic being is Lilith, whose name is based on the Hebrew word for night. Lilith is not a biblical demon; her story develops later through generations of Jewish tradition. As believers pondered the first two chapters of Genesis, they noticed that there are two stories of the creation of man and woman (Gen 1:26–28;

Gen 2:7, 21–23). In the first story man and woman seem to be created at the same time, but in the second story man seems to be created first and the woman later. In Jewish tradition the woman created in Genesis 1, who was called Lilith, asserted her independence, since she was created at the same time as Adam. So she was cast out of paradise and then God created the second woman, Eve, in Genesis 2 to replace Lilith. Lilith then becomes a night demon, seducing men and killing little children.

In the pseudepigraphical work the Apocalypse of Abraham, the one who tempts Adam and Eve to eat the fruit of the tree is called Azazel. In the Bible Azazel is the desert demon to whom the scapegoat is sent on the day of atonement (Lev 16:8, 10, 26). In 1 Enoch Azazel is accused of teaching human beings forbidden knowledge, such as the art of making war (1 Enoch 8.1; 9.6). Satan is also called Mastema (meaning "hostility" or "hatred") in the apocryphal literature (see, for example, Jubilees 10.8–11). Mastema is the one who suggests that God test Abraham by asking him to sacrifice Isaac (Jubilees 17.16).

87. So are these demons everywhere? Where do they stay?

Stories of demons indicate they could be almost anywhere, but tradition tells us that they like places where few people live, such as the desert or ruined cities. The prophet Isaiah describes the ruins of Edom as a haunt of demons, a place where no human being goes (Isa 34:8–15). The visionary of Revelation sees destroyed Babylon as a dwelling place of demons (Rev 18:2; see Isa 13:21). Most people tend to avoid these deserted places, and so the few who venture into them are often found alone and are easier targets for the devil and demons. We remember that Jesus was tempted by the devil while he was alone in the wilderness (Matt 4:1; Mark 1:13; Luke 4:2). On the other hand, people who suffer because of demons often seek out such solitary places. Because of their affliction they avoid human company or are driven out of populated areas. The man who suffered from a legion of demons lived in a burial ground (Mark 5:3). He went naked and his outbursts couldn't be restrained by anyone, so he stayed in this lonely place.

Because of this tradition, early Christian ascetics deliberately went out into the desert in order to do battle with the demons. In his story of St. Antony, St. Athanasius reports that the saint went deeper and deeper into the desert and was attacked more viciously the farther he went. But Antony prevailed over the devil and all his demons through prayer and a disciplined life. Eventually many people came to learn from his wisdom and many were freed of their own demons.

88. In Jesus' time some people were possessed by the devil or demons. Does that still happen today?

Being possessed by the devil or demons is very rare. More frequently, people are obsessed by evil spirits. In other words, they are tempted by the devil or, like St. Antony, they suffer because evil spirits afflict them from the outside with physical torments or loud noises or frightening visions. Genuine possession means that the evil spirits have taken over a person's body. The devil cannot take over a person's soul, but only the body. But, when a person is possessed, evil spirits act through that person's body. A possessed person may use terrible words, even cursing God, or do disgusting or hideous things. These words and actions are actually coming from the evil spirit that has possessed the body. Often the afflicted person does not remember any of these horrible words and actions. It is as if the spirit of the person is turned off and the demon has taken over.

Interest in demonic possession spiked in the last half of the twentieth century, spurred on by William P. Blatty's novel *The Exorcist* and its movie adaptation. People were fascinated by the story and some began to blame their difficulties on demons that supposedly possessed them. Usually their difficulties came from their own choices or simply from challenging circumstances, and not from the devil or any demon. Sometimes the person was plagued by mental illness, physical disease, or psychological trauma. Good confessors have been able to advise these sufferers regarding the reality of their situation and direct them to the counselors and doctors who could help them.

89. How do we fend off demons or the devil?

Consider how we bolster our own courage when we are afraid. Have you ever heard of whistling in the dark? In the Old Testament people who passed by a ruined city or building whistled or hissed in order to drive off the demons who might be there. For example, God warns Solomon that, if the people turn away from God, the newly dedicated temple will become a heap of ruins and every passerby will hiss (1 Kgs 9:8). The prophet Jeremiah, who lived in a time of great turmoil in Judah, knows all about whistling when one passes by ruins. The people have abandoned God, and the Mesopotamian superpower Babylon is oppressing them and threatening to invade. Jeremiah warns over and over that God will send the unfaithful people into exile and make Jerusalem and their whole land a horror, a thing to be hissed at forever (Jer 18:16; 19:8; 25:9, 18; 29:18). But he also has a message of hope. Those who destroy Jerusalem and Judah will in turn be punished for their violence. Then they in turn will become the ruins where people whistle and hiss (Jer 49:17; 50:13; 51:37).

90. Whistling seems to be only a physical reaction to danger and not an effective solution to warding off demons. Does Christian tradition give us any more help?

Yes, the Gospels give us Jesus' teaching about how to deal with demons. Matthew tells a story of the disciples' puzzlement that they cannot cast a demon out of an epileptic boy but Jesus can. When they ask why, Jesus tells them that it is because they have so little faith (Matt 17:18–20). But when Mark tells the story, Jesus says that what is necessary is prayer (Mark 9:28–29). Clearly both faith and prayer are necessary to deal with evil, especially that personified in demons. But for Christians the ultimate defense against evil is the person of Jesus. Even the name of Jesus is powerful. Shortly after the incident with the epileptic boy, the disciples discover an outsider casting out demons in the name of Jesus. The disciples, who were powerless earlier, are very upset that someone else is stealing their thunder. But Jesus reminds them that they do not have a monopoly on his name. Anyone who uses his name for good is with him (Mark 9:38–40). After the resurrection, believers are assured again that by using the name of Jesus they will cast out demons (Mark 16:17) and Paul does just that; he calls on the name of Jesus Christ to cast a demon out of a young woman in Philippi (Acts 16:18).

Many resources are available to Christians today as a defense against the devil and demons. Christ has, once for all, defeated the powers of evil. Believing in him and calling on his name is the first line of defense. The Vatican II document *Gaudium et Spes* observes that alone, we are incapable of battling the assaults of evil successfully, but Christ came to free and strengthen us and to cast out the devil who holds us captive. Prayer and frequent reception of the sacraments build a strong defense against evil. Sacramentals such as holy water, which recalls our baptism, or medals, which remind us of Christ and the saints, have traditionally been used against the power of Satan. The sign of the cross, renewing our faith in Christ's victory, is also a powerful defense against all evil. Supporting all these practices is a strong faith and a healthy prayer life. Evil is cast out only by faith and prayer.

91. What about the few people who are truly possessed by an evil spirit? Is there any help for them?

The church has a ritual called exorcism to help those who are truly possessed. It is a public ritual to drive evil spirits—Satan and/or demons—out of a person. In an exorcism the church calls upon the power of Christ to expel evil and to free persons from the grip of Satan. When it has been determined that a person is truly controlled or possessed by Satan or another evil power, a solemn exorcism may be performed. A serious investigation must be made to ensure that the problem is not an illness, whether physical or mental, but a genuine case of possession. Signs of genuine possession by an evil spirit may be superhuman strength, extraordinary knowledge of matters not easily perceived, and hatred for sacred things such as the name of God or Jesus, the sacraments, or Scripture. A solemn exorcism can be administered only by a priest designated by the bishop.

Besides the solemn exorcism in such extraordinary cases, there is also a simple exorcism that is part of the ritual of baptism. This exorcism does not imply that the person is suffering from diabolic possession; rather, its purpose is to free the person from the influence of Satan and his temptations to sin. If the candidate for baptism is old enough, he or she is asked publicly to renounce Satan and all his works. We are all in need of this strengthening against the power of evil. Thus this renunciation is repeated every year at the renewal of baptismal vows during the Easter vigil.

92. How does a priest-exorcist perform an exorcism?

A revised rite of exorcism was published in January 1999. The ritual begins as all church rituals begin, with the sign of the cross. The sufferer is sprinkled with holy water as a reminder of the exorcism in baptism. Then an appeal is made for God's mercy through the recitation of the litany of the saints and one or more psalms. A reading from the gospel is proclaimed, recalling Christ's power to expel all powers of evil. Then the priest-exorcist calls on the Holy Spirit and lays his hands on the afflicted person. He may also blow in the sufferer's face. The Apostles' Creed is recited and the person is asked to renew his or her baptismal promises and to renounce Satan and all his works. Then the Lord's Prayer is recited with its petition to deliver us from evil.

Since it is through his death and resurrection that Christ conquered evil once and for all, a crucifix is shown to the afflicted person and the sign of the cross is traced on his or her head. After a prayer, the priest-exorcist may command the evil spirit to depart. The ritual concludes with a song of thanksgiving, a prayer, and a blessing.

Friends and family of the sufferer may be present for the exorcism. They are reminded of the importance of prayer and fasting in support of the afflicted person.

93. What do the devil and demons look like, according to the Bible?

Scripture rarely describes the devil and demons. In the Old Testament imagination, demons looked like desert animals: ostriches, goats, jackals, hawks, hyenas, owls (see Isa 13:21; 34:11–14). In most of the New Testament, only those afflicted by demons are described—but not the demons themselves. The New Testament contains only one description of Satan: in the Book of Revelation, which describes Satan as the ancient serpent or the great dragon (Rev 12:9; 20:2). Thus Christian imagination has been given free reign to describe the devil.

Traditional images of the devil echo these few biblical sources. The basic form of the devil in these portrayals is human, but with extraordinary features. The goats and jackals of the Old Testament are reflected in the devil's horns, hooves, claws, and tail. Sometimes the devil has a stinger in his tail like a scorpion. The devil's scaly skin recalls the dragon or serpent of the New Testament; sometimes the dragon has multiple heads, often seven. The conviction that the devil's home is a fiery hell has contributed the red color of his skin. Some physical characteristics are given the devil simply because they are considered ugly or evil: hooked nose, glaring eyes, pointed ears. Because the devil is believed to be a spiritual being, even a fallen angel, he is given wings. He is often shown carrying a pitchfork, with which to toss the unwary into hell. Since the devil is a spirit, however, he may appear in any form, human or beast.

94. You talked about artists' descriptions of hell in the Harrowing of Hell. How do they portray Satan and the demons?

The accounts of Jesus' descent to hell or Sheol portray Satan and the demons in various ways, usually as a deathly gray color and with monstrous features. Duccio di Buoninsegna shows Satan as a hairy figure with a beard and wings. In the painting by Friedrich Pacher, Satan has a goat's head and hooves; his limbs are spiky and he has a long tail. An altarpiece painted by the Master of the Osservanza (fifteenth century) envisions the door of hell having fallen on Satan at Christ's arrival; only two hairy arms with claws are visible under the door. An engraving by Albrecht Dürer (1512) also shows Satan trapped under the fallen door, but he is a more developed figure with a dragonlike face and tongue. In Dürer's woodcut (1519) there are several demons, some with dog faces or as birds of prey. Most of them have horns, either curled or spiked; their wings are batlike and many have scales.

The biblical story of Satan's temptation of Jesus inspired artists with somewhat different images of Satan. In Botticelli's fresco, which is in the Sistine Chapel, the threefold story is told in different sections of the painting. In the first two temptations Satan is portrayed as a hermit monk, wearing a long black hooded gown with long sleeves. But he has barely visible batwings and clawed chicken-like feet. As Jesus dismisses him after the third temptation, the cloak flies off, revealing a hairy satyr-like figure with cloven feet. Paolo Veronese (sixteenth century) also portrays Satan wearing a monk's hood and cloak. Titian (ca. 1488–1576) shows Satan as a beautiful young man with curly hair offering Christ a stone to be turned into bread.

Artists use similar images in works on the last judgment. In Michelangelo's magnificent ceiling Satan has a muscular body and ears and tail like a donkey's; serpents are wound all around him. The demons also have donkey ears and horns of various shapes; many have evil grins. Fra Angelico's demons are similar, but some also have dog faces and threatening teeth. Hieronymus Bosch (ca. 1453–1516) in a triptych of the last judgment envisions demons and angels alike coming down from the sky. The demons are black-winged spider-like beings.

Donald Jackson, the artistic director of the *Saint John's Bible*, a twenty-first-century hand-illuminated, hand-calligraphied Bible, includes a red-eyed amorphous black demon waiting to tempt Jesus in his illumination for Mark 1, the baptism of Jesus. In his illumination of Matthew 16, Peter's confession, Jackson offers a horrifying modern insight into what Satan looks like. The part of the illumination that refers to Jesus' promise that the gates of hell will not prevail against the church shows Satan as a black figure with an evil, fiery face. Heads of an eagle and a horse, representing Assyrian gods, sprout out of the figure. But the most frightening part of the illumination is in the center of the figure, the microscopic image of a disease related to AIDS, a meditation on what Satan and demons look like today.

95. How do authors describe devils and demons in literature?

Writers reflect the beliefs of their time in their portrayals of Satan (the devil) and demons. In his *Divine Comedy*, written at the turn of the fourteenth century, Dante describes Satan as a horrible figure, portraying him as a giant with three faces: one red, one yellow, and one black. Two huge, bat-like wings emerge from beneath each face and tears stream from each of the six eyes. This repulsive figure is buried up to his breast in ice. In his seventeenth-century epic poem, *Paradise Lost*, John Milton presents Satan as a strong, almost heroic, figure in mortal combat with God. He refuses to accept his reality as a being created by God and claims rather that the angels (of which he is one) created themselves. In his pride, he wages war on God and is cast down with his companions into a hell of fire. Some of the fallen angels with him are Beelzebub and Belial (see question 68). His rhetorical abilities are great, so when earth is created he sets out to seduce humankind. He gives birth to sin, which sprouts from his head, and, having taken possession of a serpent, convinces Eve to eat the forbidden fruit. Adam eats willingly rather than lose Eve's companionship. Satan thinks he has won, but the Son of God intercedes for Adam and Eve. The archangel Michael is sent to expel them from Eden, but he also gives them hope by announcing the coming of a messiah.

In the nineteenth century Johann Wolfgang von Goethe wrote the drama *Faust*, based on the plot of a man selling his soul to the devil. He portrays the devil, named Mephistopheles, as a witty, sometimes sarcastic gentleman who debates with Faust about the meaning of life and the possibility of gaining happiness. At one point Faust calls him the God of the Flies, a translation of the Hebrew name Beelzebub (see question 68). Mephistopheles' method is similar to the satan in Job who, by asking questions, plants the seeds of doubt. In Job, however, the satan succeeds in making God doubt Job. In Faust, Mephistopheles succeeds in making Faust doubt God. Like Satan in *Paradise Lost*, Mephistopheles has excellent rhetorical capabilities. He consistently disguises the truth in order to make good seem evil and evil seem good. He loses his wager in the end, however, and Faust does not lose his soul.

96. Are there any recent authors who tell stories about the devil?

A couple of twentieth-century authors represent a more cynical view of the devil and demons. Stephen Vincent Benét drew on Goethe's *Faust* and a nineteenth-century story by Washington Irving called "The Devil and Tom Walker" as his sources for his short story "The Devil and Daniel Webster" (1937). A New Hampshire farmer named Jabez Stone has fallen on hard times. He sells his soul to the devil, named Mr. Scratch, in exchange for seven years of prosperity. At the end of the seven years, when the devil comes to claim his soul, the farmer appeals to Daniel Webster to defend him. Mr. Scratch wins the right to pick the judge and jury, and calls up from hell several notorious Americans. But Webster's oratory wins the day and Jabez Stone is acquitted. The devil is then banned from New Hampshire forever. The devil in Benét's story is a well-educated, smooth lawyer dressed in black. His name, Scratch, is a common term for the devil in early American culture. Irving's earlier story does not have such a happy ending. The devil, cloaked in black, reclaims the victim and carries him off on a black horse.

An English contemporary of Benét, C. S. Lewis published *The Screwtape Letters* (1942), a series of letters from a demon named Screwtape to his nephew, Wormwood. Uncle Screwtape is giving good demonic advice to Wormwood concerning the methods of deceiving and entrapping human beings and subjecting them to the rule of "Our Father Below" (Satan). Screwtape advises Wormwood to go slowly with "the Patient" to whom he is assigned, hardening his heart with bad habits. But Wormwood wants instant results and a dramatic fall into sin. Wormwood should have listened to his uncle; his plan is not successful. When the Patient is killed in an air raid, the Enemy (God) takes him to heaven. Because of his failure Wormwood is condemned to be consumed by other demons. Through this satire, Lewis presents Christian teaching from the point of view of the opposition, the demonic. The two demons are comical, but the "wisdom" Screwtape presents is a frighteningly real description of how Christians can be ensnared by sin and forget their real destiny with God.

PART FOUR

Angels in Other Traditions

97. Has the Catholic Church's teaching on angels changed since Vatican II?

No. The church, relying on the testimony of Scripture and tradition, continues to affirm the existence of angels as holy, spiritual beings who serve God and minister to humanity. In the *Catechism of the Catholic Church*, the section that speaks of angels begins with the statement: "The existence of angels—a truth of faith." The *Catechism* describes angels as glorious spiritual persons, with intelligence and will, who surpass all other creatures. Angels serve God and carry God's messages to human beings.

The *Catechism* emphasizes the angels' unique relationship to Christ. They are his angels because, along with every other thing, they were created through him and because they carry the message of his salvation. Thus they also have a special relationship to the church. Christians praise God with them and benefit from their strong protection and care. The *Catechism* supports this description of angels by recalling biblical stories of angels helping people throughout history and of the special presence of angels with Christ.

The *Catechism's* final statement about angels is a great encouragement to us: it assures us that from birth to death we are surrounded by their watchful care and intercession. Each of us is blessed with a guardian angel so even now we enjoy the companionship of the angels. Even so, what we know about angels and the joy of life with God is still very limited. The understanding of angels continues to be refined through both Jewish and Christian tradition to this present day.

98. What does modern Judaism believe about angels?

In many ways the belief in angels in contemporary Judaism is similar to that of Christianity. Like the Christian belief, it is based, first of all, on the Hebrew Scriptures and the Jewish apocrypha and pseudepigrapha. Other sources for belief are the Talmud, a collection of the wisdom of Jewish rabbis (ca. 200–500 CE) that describes the essentials of Jewish faith and prayer, and the writings from the Jewish mysticism that grew during the Middle Ages. Finally, Jewish folklore also contains many stories of people's experiences with angels and demons.

Jewish belief in angels is always conditioned by the firm conviction that there is only one God and that no creature, even an angel, can usurp God's power or claim the honor that is due only to God. Prayers are addressed only to God, never to angels. Angels are called upon to carry our prayers to God and to join us in our praise. God assigns the angels to assist human beings in matters of need, such as times of childbirth or death, famine or natural disaster. Individuals and nations have guardian angels who protect them, guide them on their way, and plead for them.

The stories of the Hasidim, a pietistic branch of Judaism that arose in Eastern Europe in the eighteenth century, illustrate the belief in angels in popular Jewish culture. One Hasidic story says that an angel teaches a baby all the wisdom of the Torah, but that another angel puts a finger on the infant's lips so that the child forgets it all before birth. Another story reveals the power of prayer. On Passover night a certain rabbi prayed so long that his whole congregation left except for one stranger, who had fallen asleep. When the rabbi saw that everyone had left, he prayed to the angels to come help him praise God. The stranger awoke to a great rushing sound and heard the rabbi recite the hymns with great joy. Some stories present an idea that contrasts with Christian belief. These stories suggest that human beings create helpful angels through their good deeds and accusing angels through their evil deeds. For example, when people said that a certain holy man had learned the melody he sang from the lips of angels, one of his disciples said that was not true; the angels, who had been born from his good deeds, had learned the melody from him.

99. Do Muslims believe in angels?

Belief in angels is a major component of Islamic belief. The Qur'an says, "The Prophet [Muhammad] believes in what has been revealed to him by his Lord, and so do the faithful. Each one believes in God and His angels, His Books and the prophets" (Sura 2.285). Belief in the angels is included in the characteristics of piety (Sura 2.177). Although angels are generally considered to be invisible, they are said to have been created from light and to have wings (Sura 35.1). The angels are "bearers of [God's] throne" and sing God's praises (Sura 40.7). They are also active as intermediaries between God and human beings, begging forgiveness for those who have fallen (Sura 42.5). They are guardian angels: God "has power over His creatures, and appoints guardians to watch over them. When death comes to one of you, our messengers take away his soul" (Sura 6.61). Each person is said to have two angels "who keep the account, one sitting on the right, one on the left." These angels will report every word on the day of judgment (Sura 50:16–28).

The Qur'an mentions four archangels: Gabriel, Michael, Israfil, and the Angel of Death, sometimes called Azrael. Gabriel is the one who reveals God's word to the prophets and who revealed the Qur'an to Muhammad (Sura 2.97). Presumably Gabriel is the angel who reveals God's plan to Zechariah and to Mary (Sura 19.7–9, 17–21). Islamic tradition also names Gabriel as Muhammad's guide when he ascends to heaven. Azrael, the angel of death, is the one who sounds the trumpet on the last day, the day of resurrection. On that day eight angels will carry God's throne when he comes for judgment (Sura 69.15–18).

According to the Qur'an, human beings rank higher than the angels, because God has given them the gift of knowledge (Sura 2.30–33). When God "asked the angels to bow in homage to Adam, they all bowed but Iblis" (Sura 2:34), who said, "I am better than him. You created me from fire and him from clay" (Sura 7.12). So Iblis is thrown into hell with all those who follow him (Sura

7.13–18). This story is similar to the tradition about the fall of Satan (see question 64).

100. Do people still have experiences with angels?

Every so often I ask someone, "Have you ever had an experience of an angel?" The first response tends to be a look that says, "Are you crazy? Do you think I'm crazy?" But the second reaction is almost always a story that begins, "I haven't told anyone about this. But this happened to me." Sometimes their stories have to do with angels encouraging them to do a kind deed for someone in need. Some stories have to do with protection from an unseen danger. Angels seem to be particularly active in situations of sickness and death.

The sisters in my community frequently comment on the presence of angels when a sister is dying. The nurses too know when the angels are there. One night an elderly sister was very agitated because she knew the angels were present and she was not ready to die. Another sister died that night. A few months later the angels came back for the first sister, who was now much more peaceful.

101. Why is there so much interest in angels today?

American society has certainly discovered angels. Books about angels can be found everywhere, from church vestibules to airport kiosks. Angels appear on TV and in the movies. A Gallup poll taken in May 2007 indicated that 75 percent of Americans believe in angels. Seventy percent report that they believe in the devil. Many faithful people wear angel pins to remind them to call on the protection of angels. Portraits of angels from medieval, baroque, romantic, and modern art are found on calendars and cards.

Why are angels so popular today? Belief in angels may be a reaction to our materialistic and secular culture that endangers spiritual values. Increasing awareness of the great evils that afflict the world today may be another catalyst that draws believers to a hope in spiritual beings who can help us live well and lead us to God. Just possibly angels have become so popular because they are very active among us. They may know how much help we need! May the angels protect everyone who reads this book!

Notes

(The notes are numbered according to the questions and answers.)

2. *Catechism of the Catholic Church* (Rome: Libreria Editrice Vaticana, 1994), questions 327–36, 350–53.

7. James H. Charlesworth, ed., *The Old Testament Pseudepigrapha*, 2 vols. (Garden City, NY: Doubleday, 1983, 1985) 1.5–315, esp.. 4–12, 92–100, 223–54.

8. Ibid., 2.35–142, 249–95.

9. See *Catechism*, question 327; St. Thomas Aquinas, *Summa Theologica*, 3 vols., translated by the Fathers of the English Dominican Province (New York: Benziger, 1947–48) 1.61.3. The decree *Dei Filius* is available online at http://www.ewtn.com/library/COUNCILS/V1.htm#4.

10. Aquinas, *Summa Theologica* 1.50.3.

11. St. Augustine, Ps 103:4, no. 1, par. 15, *Expositions on the Psalms*, translated by Maria Boulding, OSB (New York: New City Press, 2003), vol. 5, 125.

18. St. Jerome, "Commentary on Matthew" Matt 18:10; *Corpus Christianorum* 77; St. Basil, "Homily 16: On Psalm 33[34]"; Aquinas, *Summa Theologica* 1.113.2, 4; 1.108.7; St. Ambrose, "On Widows," 9.55, *Nicene and Post-Nicene Fathers* 10.

26. Charlesworth, *Old Testament Pseudepigrapha* 1.865–66; 1.514.

32. St. Jerome, "Homily 58 on Psalm 48," *Fathers of the Church* 48; St. Gregory the Great, "Homily 34 on Luke 15:1–10," *Gregory the Great: Forty Gospel Homilies*, translated by David Hurst (Kalamazoo, MI: Cistercian Publications, 1990), Homily 34, pars. 7–14; Aquinas, *Summa Theologica*, 1.108.1–2.

35. Qumran Hymn of Thanksgiving 14, lines 12–13; 1QH 14.12–13.

39. *Sibylline Oracles*, Book 2, line 215; Charlesworth, *Old Testament Pseudepigrapha* 1.350.

46. St. Ambrose, "To Horantianus," Letter 51, *Fathers of the Church* 26, 276; "To Irenaeus," Letter 85, *Fathers of the Church* 26, 479–80.

47. St. Augustine, *Expositions on the Psalms* Ps 118/119:73 no. 18, par. 4; vol. 5, 427–28.

51. Dante Alighieri, *Divine Comedy: Paradiso*, Canto 28; Shakespeare, *Macbeth*, act 4, scene 3; *Hamlet*, act 1, scene 4; *Romeo and Juliet*, act 2, scene 2; *Hamlet*, act 5, scene 2; John Donne, "Holy Sonnets" 7; John Milton, *Paradise Lost*, books 4–5, 7, 10[12].

52. Andrew M. Greeley, *Angel Light: An Old-Fashioned Love Story* (New York: Tom Doherty Associates, 1995); Frederick Buechner, *On the Road with the Archangel* (San Francisco: Harper San Francisco, 1997).

56. St. Augustine, "To Evodius," Letter 159, *Fathers of the Church*, 20.363–67.

61. See *Catechism of the Catholic Church*, question 391.

62. *Life of Adam and Eve* 11–17, Charlesworth, *Old Testament Pseudepigrapha* 2.260–64; Origen, *De principiis* 1.5.4, *Ante-Nicene Fathers* 4.

66. *Life of Adam and Eve* 15–19, Charlesworth, *Old Testament Pseudepigrapha* 2.262–64.

72. Johann Wolfgang von Goethe, *Faust* (1808, 1832), part 1, scene 21; part 2, act 2, scene 3.

77. See *Gaudium et Spes*, par. 2.

80. See *Catechism of the Catholic Church*, 631–37.

82. Dante Alighieri, *Divine Comedy: Inferno*.

83. St. Benedict, *Rule of Benedict: RB 1980*, edited by Timothy Fry et al. (Collegeville, MN: Liturgical Press, 1981).

84. St. Basil, "On Envy," *Patrologia Graeca* 31. 372–81; see Vasiliki Limberis, "The Eyes Infected by Evil: Basil of Caesarea's Homily, *On Envy*," HTR 84, no. 2 (1991): 163–84.

86. *Apocalypse of Abraham* 23, Charlesworth, *Old Testament Pseudepigrapha* 700.

87. St. Athanasius, *The Life of Antony and the Letter to Marcellinus*, Classics of Western Spirituality, translated by Robert C. Gregg (New York/Mahwah, NJ: Paulist Press, 1980), 29–129.

88. William Peter Blatty, *The Exorcist* (New York: Harper & Row, 1971). Movie version, 1973.

90. *Gaudium et Spes*, par. 13.

91. *Catechism of the Catholic Church*, questions 1237, 1673.

92. *BCL Newsletter* (January-February 1999).

95. Dante Alighieri, *Divine Comedy: Inferno*, canto 34; John Milton, *Paradise Lost*, book 5.

95. Johann Wolfgang von Goethe, *Faust*.

96. Stephen Vincent Benét, "The Devil and Daniel Webster" in *Thirteen O'Clock: Stories of Several Worlds* (New York/Toronto: Farrar & Rinehart; 1937); C. S. Lewis, *The Screwtape Letters* (London: G. Bles, 1942).

97. *Catechism of the Catholic Church*, 328–36.

98. Martin Buber, *Tales of the Hasidim: Early Masters* (New York: Schocken Books, 1973) 95–96, 207, 297; see also 247.

99. Jaroslav Pelikan, ed., *Sacred Writings*, vol. 3, *Islam: The Qur'an*, translated by Ahmed Ali (New York: QPB, 1992).

Additional Bibliography

Anchor Bible Dictionary. Ed. David Noel Freedman. New York: Doubleday, 1992.

Angels: The Concept of Celestial Beings—Origins, Development and Reception. Deuterocanonical and Cognate Literature Yearbook 2007. Edited by Friedrich V. Reiterer, Tobias Nicklas, Karin Schöpflin. Berlin/New York: Walter de Gruyter, 2007.

Collegeville Pastoral Dictionary of Biblical Theology. Edited by Carroll Stuhlmueller. Collegeville, MN: Liturgical Press, 1994.

Dictionary of Deities and Demons in the Bible. 2d edition. Edited by Karel van der Toorn, Bob Becking, Pieter W. Van der Horst. Grand Rapids, MI: William B. Eerdmans, 1999.

Encyclopaedia Judaica. Jerusalem, 1972.

Isaacs, Ronald H. *Ascending Jacob's Ladder: Jewish Views of Angels, Demons, and Evil Spirits*. Northvale, NJ, and Jerusalem: Jason Aronson, 1998.

Margolies, Morris B. *A Gathering of Angels: Angels in Jewish Life and Literature*. Northvale, NJ, and Jerusalem: Jason Aronson, 1994, 2000.

New Catholic Encyclopedia. New York: McGraw-Hill, 1967.

New Dictionary of Catholic Spirituality. Edited by Michael Downey. Collegeville, MN: Liturgical Press, 1993.

New Dictionary of Theology. Edited by Joseph Komonchak, Mary Collins, Dermot Lane. Wilmington, DE: Michael Glazier, 1987.

New Interpreter's Dictionary of the Bible. Vols. 1–2. Nashville, TN: Abingdon, 2006, 2007.

Theological Dictionary of the New Testament. Edited by Gerhard Kittel and Gerhard Friedrich. Translated by Geoffrey W. Bromiley. Grand Rapids, MI: Eerdmans, 1964–76.

Vermes, Geza, ed. *The Complete Dead Sea Scrolls in English*. New York: Allen Lane Penguin Press, 1997.

Other Books in This Series

101 QUESTIONS AND ANSWERS ON THE BIBLE
by Raymond E. Brown, SS

101 QUESTIONS AND ANSWERS ON THE BIBLICAL TORAH
by Roland E. Murphy, O Carm

101 QUESTIONS AND ANSWERS ON THE CHURCH
by Richard P. McBrien

101 QUESTIONS AND ANSWERS ON CONFUCIANISM, DAOISM, AND SHINTO
by John Renard

101 QUESTIONS AND ANSWERS ON DEACONS
by William T. Ditewig

101 QUESTIONS AND ANSWERS ON ISLAM
by John Renard

101 QUESTIONS AND ANSWERS ON PAUL
by Ronald D. Witherup

101 QUESTIONS AND ANSWERS ON VATICAN II
by Maureen Sullivan, OP

101 QUESTIONS AND ANSWERS ON CATHOLIC MARRIAGE PREPARATION
by Rebecca Nappi and Daniel Kendall, SJ

101 QUESTIONS AND ANSWERS ON THE FOUR LAST THINGS
by Joseph T. Kelley

101 QUESTIONS AND ANSWERS ON THE EUCHARIST
by Giles Dimock, OP

101 QUESTIONS AND ANSWERS ON CATHOLIC MARRIED LIFE
by Catherine Johnston; Daniel Kendall, SJ; and Rebecca Nappi

101 QUESTIONS AND ANSWERS ON SAINTS
by George P. Evans

101 QUESTIONS AND ANSWERS ON POPES AND THE PAPACY
by Christopher M. Bellitto

101 QUESTIONS AND ANSWERS ON PRAYER
by Joseph T. Kelley

101 QUESTIONS AND ANSWERS ON THE HISTORICAL BOOKS OF THE BIBLE
by Victor H. Matthews

101 QUESTIONS AND ANSWERS ON THE SACRAMENTS OF HEALING
by Paul Jerome Keller, OP

101 QUESTIONS AND ANSWERS ON *THE DA VINCI CODE* AND THE CATHOLIC TRADITION
by Nancy de Flon and John Vidmar, OP

101 QUESTIONS AND ANSWERS ON EASTERN CATHOLIC CHURCHES
by Edward Faulk

101 QUESTIONS AND ANSWERS ON THE PROPHETS OF ISRAEL
by Victor H. Matthews

Other Books
Under the Former Series Title

RESPONSES TO 101 QUESTIONS ON THE DEAD SEA SCROLLS
by Joseph A. Fitzmyer, SJ

RESPONSES TO 101 QUESTIONS ABOUT JESUS
by Michael L. Cook, SJ

RESPONSES TO 101 QUESTIONS ON THE PSALMS AND OTHER WRITINGS
by Roland E. Murphy, O Carm

RESPONSES TO 101 QUESTIONS ON DEATH AND ETERNAL LIFE
by Peter C. Phan

RESPONSES TO 101 QUESTIONS ON HINDUISM
by John Renard

RESPONSES TO 101 QUESTIONS ON BUDDHISM
by John Renard

RESPONSES TO 101 QUESTIONS ON THE MASS
by Kevin W. Irwin

RESPONSES TO 101 QUESTIONS ON GOD AND EVOLUTION
by John F. Haught

RESPONSES TO 101 QUESTIONS ON CATHOLIC SOCIAL TEACHING
by Kenneth R. Himes, OFM